Transforming
Society's Failure

Omari Amili

NOV 0 3 2017

NO LONGER PROPERTY OF
SEATTLE PUBLIC LIBRARY

NOV 0 3 2017

Copyright © 2017 Omari Amili
http://www.ProgressionWA.com
http://www.OmariAmili.com
Contact: ProgressionWA@gmail.com
Cover art by Gabriel Campanario of The Seattle Times
All rights reserved.

ISBN: 1544744676
ISBN-13: 978-1544744674

DEDICATION

This book is dedicated to my family and friends, especially those who are no longer with us. I love you guys!

I also dedicate this book to anyone who might be reading it from inside of a prison or jail. Don't wait until you get out to be the best you that you can be! There are no limits to our potential unless we set them ourselves. You will be successful if you are willing to put the work in!

CONTENTS

1
EARLY CHILDHOOD

What does it mean to hit a lick? Well, there are a lot of things you can do that fit the definition. The main thing is that it's a come up. You got something for nothing. You obtained some money or something of value and it wasn't from working.

I first heard the term in the early 90's when my mom and step dad would talk about going into stores stealing. They would always say, "let's go hit a lick", or, "did you hit that lick?" They would take me and my sisters with them with no hesitation on their mission to steal. The things they would steal the most are cartons of cigarettes and batteries from big groceries stores. They would sell them to smaller corner stores to get money for drugs. Would it be a surprise to anyone if this helped shape my views toward stealing as a kid?

I was born in Seattle, Washington on March 23rd, 1985. I was the third of my mom's four kids and the fourth of my dad's six. Well, with my dad you never know. He had a way with women and often talked about other kids that could have been his, even one who became a multi-millionaire star basketball player whose mother he once dated.

My dad, Frelimo, was a former member of the Black Panthers from Vancouver, Washington. At the time of my birth he was working and he had his shit together. His birth name was Freddy Mitchell Withlow, but he didn't want to keep his "slave name" so he changed it to Frelimo Albert Amili, during young adulthood. Frelimo is an acronym for the Portuguese term Frente de Libertação de Moçambique, meaning Front for the Liberation of Mozambique. My dad was known for being anti-authority and very rebellious. He was

1

also known by many as the smartest man they had ever met.

My mom came from a more privileged background than my dad did. Her parents were married with four children. My dad's mom, on the other hand, had double the amount of kids. That alone can lead to a drastically different upbringing.

My mom was born in St. Paul, Minnesota and moved to Portland, Oregon when she was very young. The transition from St. Paul to Portland would not happen without struggle for her nuclear family. My grandpa, Rowan Wiley, and my grandma, Parthina, had to go through a lot to have a home in a nice neighborhood to raise their kids in.

My grandma was a black woman but she was very light skinned with red hair. Due to racial discrimination, my grandparents realized that they would get better results if my grandma was the face of the purchasing family and if she went into the banks to apply for home loans rather than my grandpa. I learned that this was a common thing that black people had to do to get by called "passing". There have been books written about it including Nella Larsen's *Passing* and James Weldon Johnson's *The Autobiography of an Ex-Colored Man*. From my experience, when you hear of people in your own family doing this, the reality hits a lot harder. My grandma conducted the business involved with purchasing the land and having a home built. Everything would go smoothly until they saw my grandpa and found out the family was black.

The banks, realty companies, and construction companies flat out refused to work fairly with my grandparents once they found out they were black. Because their ethnicity was the only basis for being denied a home, my grandparents had no choice but to turn to the courts for litigation. The Fair Housing Act was enacted in Oregon in 1959 and my grandparents were the first people to call upon the law in 1960. My grandparents won a lawsuit that required the bank, the realty company, and the construction company to work fairly with them. However, by the time the court had made the decision, my grandparents had already closed on land in an all-white neighborhood called Park Rose.

My grandparents finally had the land in a neighborhood they liked and they began building. Happily ever after right? Of course not, remember this is an all-white neighborhood in 1960. One day my grandparents went to check on the progress of the construction of their new home and they were spotted by some of their new neighbors. The neighbors organized and came up with a plan to stop my black grandparents and their black kids from infiltrating their white neighborhood. Not much time passed before the Richland Water District used their power to rule that my grandparents' house violated regulations and tried to force them to sell their property. My grandparents wanted to negotiate but that didn't work so they went right back to court. Once again my grandparents won, the Richland Water District's blatant discrimination had failed, and progress could continue with making their new residence a reality.

Ok, so now, happily ever after, right? Nope! Not even one month after the judge ruled in my grandparents' favor, another attempt was made at stopping them from moving into the all-white community of Park Rose. On July 3rd, 1960, the day before we celebrate freedom and independence, a racist arsonist set their house on fire in a last ditch effort to ensure that the neighborhood remain segregated. The fire caused thousands upon thousands of dollars in damage.

My grandparents were determined at this point and they had already owned the land which was the biggest hurdle. This house was going to be built! They didn't let the racist arsonists stop them. They immediately began rebuilding and within months construction was complete.

My mom grew up in this house and it stayed in the family up until the 1990s after both of my grandparents died. The thing I remember most about the house is the swimming pool in the back yard. I never had another family member or even a friend here in the Northwest that had a real swimming pool in the backyard of their house. I wish that house was still in our family, considering what my grandparents had to go through in order to build it. I will never forget that house.

My grandpa died in 1989 and my grandma died on Mother's Day in 1990. Although I was only five at the time I can remember being in the backseat of the car when my grandmother began to have the heart attack that killed her. That is one car ride I will never forget. I wish I had more time with my grandparents.

Around the time I was born, my mom and dad both were holding down good jobs and providing for their family which included them, my oldest sister Nikki, my other older sister Sareeta and me. Nikki, who is seven years older than me, is my half-sister. We have the same mom but not the same dad. Sareeta is three years older than I am, she is my mom and dad's first child together, but she has a hyphenated combination of both of their last names because our parents weren't married when she was born. They didn't decide to get married until they found out my mom was pregnant with me. We had a house to live in and food on the table. Life was great, as far as I know.

My younger sister, Yakini, was born three years after I was in 1988. By the time she was born crack cocaine abuse had spread throughout the black community and caused tremendous problems for our family. Eventually my mom and dad got divorced and we moved from the Central District of Seattle to Northeast Portland, Oregon with our mom.

My dad stayed in Seattle at first but he eventually became a transient going back-and-forth between Portland, Vancouver and Seattle. His life had been dominated by drug and alcohol abuse. My dad never worked again after him and my mom split up. He never paid a dime of child support. However, he never gave up on being a father to his kids.

My mom also had a problem with crack cocaine. Moving to Portland did not stop this. Her habit continued and she eventually met her second husband, Fred. It was weird for me and my sisters to see our mom with another man. However, it wasn't long before they were living together and eventually married.

Together those two weren't the best parents. They loved us but their addiction messed their priorities up. The houses we lived in would always become crack houses. My mom and Fred would allow their dealers to stay in our house to sell to them and all their friends. The dealers would eventually start having other random people come meet them at our house who we didn't even know and the traffic was non-stop.

I never thought anything of it. I never thought about the fact that they were bad parents and I wasn't being raised right. I didn't know that things completely out of my control as a child were already laying the foundation for me to be a failure in adulthood. A lot of the drug dealers were nice to me so I wasn't bothered by their presence.

When I was seven I taught myself how to do backflips, cartwheels and other types of tumbling. I was a daredevil and I would flip off of anything. I once flipped off the roof of a garage just because someone dared me to do it. Some of the drug dealers that set up shop in my house would give me money to do flips. I remember one of them would give me a dollar for each consecutive back handspring I could do without stopping. How cool is that to do something I want to do anyway and get paid for it? I never had a problem with any of the drug dealers who would come around and they all seemed to like me and want to give me money. Why wouldn't I want these guys around?

I remember the first time I saw my mom "hit a lick" so that she could pay for drugs. It was during a period in the early 90's when we were living in Portland. I think she might have liked having a kid with her so that she wouldn't look suspicious. She took me with her and Fred to the grocery store and when we got there Fred stayed in the car with it running. My mom took me inside the store with her. When we went in I watched my mom stuff her over-sized purse with several cartons of cigarettes and then she grabbed a bunch of name-brand double-A batteries and put those in her purse as well. We went through the register like any other paying customers but she only paid for a can of pop. We walked out of the store as if nothing happened but we were followed out by an employee.

"Ma'am stop!", The employee yelled from right behind us.

My mom grabbed my hand and we ran to the car where Fred was waiting to speed off. I remember being scared to death. They drove straight to a small corner store to sell the goods and then straight to the dope man so they could get high.

Speaking of my mom's over-sized purse. She was the buffet's worst nightmare! Before we would go to the buffet my mom would always put some zip lock bags and plastic grocery bags in her purse. Once we get to the restaurant my mom will eat a little bit here and there but most her time was spent filling up the bags making sure to fit as much food as she could in her purse. She would even do this at smaller restaurants like Skippers that might only have one item she could take such as all-you-can-eat shrimp. We would come home with who knows how many pounds of food that would last us through the week before finally we end up throwing the scraps away.

There were many times when we didn't have a place to live due to either getting evicted or some other unfortunate circumstance that was the result of my mom and Fred's addiction. There was once a time when we were in-between homes, essentially homeless, and staying in a cheap motel on MLK in Portland. My mom and Fred went to hit licks with a family friend from Seattle and didn't come back that night. Nikki wasn't even around but they left me, Yakini, and Sareeta in the motel room with the family friend's two daughters. The night after they left we were watching the news…

"Breaking news tonight out of Northeast Portland. A woman was killed instantly when the car she was in collided with a tree. The car was fleeing from officers after the people inside were supposedly shoplifting cartons of cigarettes", the news anchor announced.

Sitting there in that motel room I saw an old mugshot of our family friend from Seattle, who had left yesterday with our parents, flash across the screen. Then, as if to confirm it was truly her, the news anchor said her name. Her children and Yakini were too young to fully comprehend what had happened but me and Sareeta began crying.

All I could think about was, "where could my mom and step dad possibly be?" Were they in the car too? Were they also dead? What would happen with her daughters? Am I going to die?

Eventually my mom and Fred came back and we found out they were fine. Neither one of them were there that night when their friend had died. I felt so relieved to still have my mom but I felt so bad for those poor kids who no longer did. They were now orphans because their dad had been killed a couple years prior. I never saw them again after that. Even these types of dramatic events didn't lead to a lifestyle change for my mom and Fred. They just went deeper and deeper into their addiction.

Sometimes we would end up with my dad for a few days. He would come get us and take us on all kinds of adventures. My dad was mostly homeless and didn't have a job so there were times that we would be outside in the dark, fighting the cold, trying to figure out where we would sleep for the night. My dad's go-to spot when he couldn't find a relative or friend to let us sleep over was Mr. Buchannan's car. Me, my dad, Yakini and Sareeta would all sleep in the car together in front of Mr. Buchanan's house. Although Mr. Buchanan wouldn't let us sleep inside he always gave us enough blankets to stay warm.

It sounds cold blooded of Mr. Buchanan to have us sleep in the car rather than in his house but we had dealt with complete rejection so many times that we considered this to be very generous of him. We appreciated having the car to sleep in when there was nowhere else. My dad would have us look at the stars and point out constellations to us. He had stories he would tell us and silly songs he would sing to keep us entertained.

Although my dad did not work or have much money he would always preach to us the importance of knowledge, being articulate, and having manners. Despite his low social-standing he strived to teach his kids to have class. He sure had some interesting ways of teaching us though. I remember being hit if I would put my elbows on the table while I was eating if I was around him.

My dad always gave me magazines like the Reader's Digest and National Geographic to read when I was with him. I was a very advanced reader at a young age thanks to him. He also took us to places like the grotto and the zoo where we had educational experiences rather than just having fun. He never had the money to pay for us to do these things so most of the time we would sneak in.

Sometimes when we were with my dad we would end up pan-handling with him. He had no shame asking complete strangers for spare change and when we were with him we did it to. It was necessary for us to eat a lot of the time. There were even times when other homeless pan-handlers had given us money out of concern for seeing a father and his kids out there.

Whenever I think about us pan-handling I always picture us out in the U-District in Seattle. There were times when my dad would take us from Portland to Seattle on the Greyhound without my mom's permission with no plans to bring us back. I remember being out there right near the University of Washington campus walking around asking people for spare change. I always wondered where all the people walking by were going. I wished that one day I would be a student at the University of Washington so I could play basketball.

We were never with my dad long but he was always very resourceful when we were. He taught us to go to pizza restaurants and ask if there were any "mistakes" or orders that hadn't been picked up that we could have. Instead of throwing the pizza away sometimes the manager would be kind enough to give them away. This worked for us a lot and pizza was my favorite food growing up. My dad also knew where to go to get bus tickets and random vouchers that could help us. Sometimes it would be food vouchers, sometimes clothing vouchers, other times even a motel voucher. He would always do his best to make sure we were ok when we were with him.

Although my dad was an atheist he would often go to churches for help. He was even willing to work to get what he needed for us. I remember him doing yard work at a church in exchange for a meal and a motel room for us for a night. When we weren't with him he had no problem sleeping at a bus stop or a park bench but he didn't do that when he had us. I used to worry about him a lot and wonder if I would ever see him again every time he brought us back to our mom.

One time when my dad took us from our mom he actually got an apartment for us in Seattle. That was a major upgrade from the abandoned house with no electricity in Portland that we were living in with him the time before. Unfortunately, it didn't last long. My dad took me, Yakini and Sareeta to see Bruce Lee's grave site and afterwards we stopped at a grocery store on Broadway. Outside of the store my dad had yelled at me about something, I was always full of energy and bouncing all over the place so it could have been anything. Inside the store my dad bought us some candy and we went to look at the newspapers on the way out. In Seattle there were two major newspapers at the time and my dad had one of them in his back pocket when we came into the store. He had only looked at the other paper that he didn't have already, yet he was accused of stealing the newspaper that was in his back pocket.

My dad is not the type to cooperate when he is being wrongfully accused. The workers began to ask him questions about when he had yelled at me outside the store. Apparently one of the employees was outside on a smoke break when it happened. When they decided to question my dad about his kids he started calling them "crackers" and "peckerwoods" and accusing them of racial profiling. Some people might say that it's hypocritical to use those terms while accusing someone else of being racist but he is one of many black people of his generation who have been victims of racial injustice their whole life. Just like so many other times when he didn't deserve it, this situation ended with my dad being taken to jail.

When my dad went to jail we had nowhere to go. Apparently, he had some old warrants and he wasn't going to get right out. We were turned over to Child Protective Services and sent to foster care until my mom found out where we were and came and got us.

There were two times in the early 90's when me and my sisters ended up in foster care. The second time my mom and Fred had abandoned us at a motel again. They had just come up on a bit of money so they paid the motel for a week, left, and this time they never came back for us. Nikki was off doing her own thing, despite her young age, so me, Sareeta, and Yakini were all alone with no one to take care of us. Eventually after the week was up a motel employee called CPS because he hadn't seen our parents and we were taken in to their custody. We didn't want to be split up but we had no choice. Me and Yakini were sent to one couple's house, while Sareeta was sent somewhere else. We didn't stay in the foster home for long but it was longer than the first time, and long enough to be registered in a new school. After a while my mom and Fred found a new place for us to live and we went home to them.

Fresh out of CPS custody, it wasn't long before we once again lived in a crack house. Eventually our new house was just like the previous ones; Full of drug dealers and drug addicts and no environment to raise children. My mom and Fred managed to run up a huge debt to one of the more dangerous drug dealers that would come around. With no way to pay him we were forced to abandon our house and leave with whatever we could grab in the middle of the night. All of our lives were threatened and my mom and Fred knew this guy well enough to take that threat very seriously. We packed up and moved across the Interstate Bridge to Vancouver. This wasn't far away at all but most gangsters don't leave the hood and it wouldn't be easy for him to find us.

When we first moved to Vancouver we were staying at a motel but eventually my mom and Fred found a shelter for us to stay in. After being forced to run for their lives my mom and Fred decided that maybe they should clean up their act. After living in Vancouver for a couple months my mom decided that we should move back to Seattle and Fred was with it.

2
THE MOVE

We moved back to Seattle during the early months of 1995 when I was just about to turn 10-years old. My mom was able to find a shelter for us to live at called Seattle Emergency Housing. I was happy because moving back to the Central District allowed us to be close to family on my dad's side.

Although none of Fred or my mom's family lived in Seattle, my dad had family there. His brother lived in the CD with his wife. They had a son and two daughters together and his wife also had two sons from a previous marriage. Her sister also lived nearby. She had two sons and a daughter. These guys are the family members that I was closest to outside of our household.

I was especially close to my cousins Mak and Jay. I am younger than Mak by two years and Jay by three years. After moving back to Seattle I was always with them doing whatever they were doing. I didn't grow up with any boys in the household so I always viewed and treated my cousins more like my brothers. Plus, I looked up to them.

One of the main things I had in common with Jay and Mak was a love for basketball. We used to hoop every day. Eventually we came to have our hustle in common. Most 10, 12 and 13 year olds don't know anything out hustling but because of our disadvantaged upbringing we weren't prevented from getting any early start. Our desire to hustle was born out of necessity.

At 10 years old I gave myself the nickname O.G. Hustler. It was a joke but it actually stuck for a while. I was always the youngest person in the crowd but I would say that I was probably the most advanced in most things we did because I was always a thinker and an observer. I learned a lot of from my older cousins' mistakes because they were a lot more impulsive than I was.

Leaning on what I had witnessed from my mom and Fred, combined with the game and influence I soaked up from my cousins, I became a thief and a con artist. At first, I would only steal petty stuff like candy. Eventually I graduated to shoes, clothes, and other more useful and expensive things. Being a thief was an everyday thing, but I also needed money as well.

Mak's oldest brother, Mega, had a friend that introduced us to a hustle that changed our childhoods. We went to downtown Seattle with him to see it in action one day and we were hooked. What he would do was not much different than what I used to do when I would pan-handle with my dad. We would walk up to complete strangers and ask them for money. The difference was we weren't asking for the money for ourselves, we were doing it in the name of a fabricated charitable organization called the "All the Way Right Program".

When we were first introduced to "All the Way Right" no one else in the city was doing it. After we started making a lot of money and telling our friends, countless young poor black kids, from the Central District, the South End, and the West Side, began doing it and now had a way to make an easy 20-50 dollars an hour on average. What you make you keep, there was nobody splitting money or taking cuts.

Making this hustle a trend was nothing that we did intentionally and there was absolutely no organization or structure to it. However, slowly, but surely, it spread. I always considered myself to be a pioneer because it seems like every time we found a new hustle it wasn't long before it spread around the whole city.

When me, Jay and Mak were first introduced to "All the Way Right" our documentation was a single sheet of white paper with one poorly articulated paragraph on it. The sheet of paper was laminated at Kinko's Copy and that's all we needed to hit the streets and collect money. We would approach anyone who walked by, show them the paper and say whatever popped up in our head. Eventually we started to think about ways to improve it and make more money.

Our additions included trading the laminated single sheet of paper for a folder with the paper stapled to one side and a sheet for our "donors" to write their name and the amount on the other. We often got asked questions about whether or not the donation was tax-deductible or for details about the location of our operations and we could always bullshit our way through the conversation.

One day we were at a family friend named Terry's house and Terry was the only person we knew who had a computer. Encouraged by Jay and Mak I sat down and began typing a new and improved version of "All the Way Right". Because "All the Way Right" was someone else's idea and there were some other people using it by then, I decided that the new version I created should have a new name. I came up with the name "Washington's Positive Teens". I typed out a full page describing an organization that aimed to support at-risk youth and help keep them off of the streets. Me, Jay and Mak came up with fake names for ourselves and created set speeches for consistency. I can still remember my speech…

"Excuse me sir, my name is Jeffrey, from Washington's Positive Teens, an organization focused on keeping at-risk teens off the street. Right now our main focus is collecting donations for a three-on-three basketball tournament that will take place on the weekends when 98% of crime takes place. If you could find it in your heart to please donate it would be greatly appreciated, even a dollar would help."

I have gotten everything from pennies to hundred dollar bills from complete strangers thanks to this speech and the paper I had written. All of a sudden I was making more money at 10-11 years old than most adults had the potential to make on an hourly basis unless they had a really good job. I never cared about the fact that I was lying saying the money was going to charitable causes. I was dirt poor. I never felt that I was doing anything wrong. When my dad would pan-handle a lot of the money would go on alcohol but he wasn't going to come out and say that. From my limited and distorted perspective, it was normal to lie to get what you want. I was simply doing what I had to do. Eventually this would come to be known as "hitting the huss". One day I will make the organization we pretended to be a part of a reality as a way to make amends to all of the people I got over on.

When me, Jay, and Mak weren't hitting the huss after school we were more than likely either playing basketball or stealing clothes. None of us went to the same school or lived together but we would still see each other almost every day. We would always meet up after school at Wendy's downtown and sometimes we would even plan to skip school to get an early start.

There was a time when I was a 5th grader at Bailey Gatzert Elementary and I skipped and went to Meany Magnet School to see if I could sneak along on Jay's field trip. When Jay went in to his class I stayed outside. The plan was to try to blend in when they were loading up on the bus.

Jay was in the 8th grade at the time, so his whole class was obviously a lot bigger than I was, but somehow when they came out and lined up for the bus I was able to blend right in. I got on the bus just like everyone else and I rode with them all the way to the Puyallup fair. I was given a bracelet to get on rides on my way off the bus and everything. Me and Jay spent the whole day and the whole night there at the fair going on rides and doing all kinds of other fun stuff. We completely lost track of time and the school bus left and went back to Seattle without us. You would think they would have refused to leave without every child being accounted for. We ended up stranded once the fair closed and we had no choice but to approach a police officer and tell him what happened.

The police officers called our parents and agreed to drop us off back in Seattle. As I am writing this I have a son in the 5th grade and I would be completely furious if he was allowed on a school bus when he wasn't even a student at the school. I would be even more furious that they left him in Puyallup! This is just one of many ways I have been failed by the Seattle Public School district in my lifetime. I made poor decisions but there should have been some sort of protections in place.

By this time I had gotten used to doing whatever I wanted without the need for permission. Hitting the huss took us all over downtown Seattle and we were used to being unsupervised. The lack of supervision opened the door for more criminal activity. We started making our way into more and more stores downtown, just passing through and browsing. Soon enough, we were going into those stores to steal clothes. Although we would steal from a lot of stores, the main store that we hit up was Eddie Bauer. I don't know what it was that attracted us to Eddie Bauer but that store was always a target of ours.

I never felt like I was doing anything wrong when I stole from stores. Despite our willingness to steal from stores, we never stole from people. We were not completely without values we just had values that were distorted by the reality of our upbringing.

To be honest I don't know how we got away with stealing all of the clothes we stole. Here I am, a 10-year-old boy, walking into this store with two early teenagers and we all have an empty backpack on. The only thing in our backpacks to start the day would be our huss paper.

We walked around the store grabbing armfuls of clothes that we took into the changing room to "try on". We would fill up our bags and when our bags got full we would put more items on under our clothes that we were wearing. We made sure to get everything we liked the most in our own size but it didn't matter too much because we could always exchange the stuff without presenting a receipt. From time to time, employees would ask if we need assistance or follow us around the store but it was still rare for us to get caught. They had to notice how stuffed our once-empty backpacks were upon leaving the dressing room, however, we usually just walked right out the store with no issue. Whenever they did try to stop us we would just run, and due to the fact that they couldn't touch us, we would usually get away.

There were times that I did get caught but it was always when I didn't run. I got caught at The Bon stealing Sonics jerseys with my sister Sareeta, I got caught at Bartell's Drugs stealing a calculator with Jay, and I got caught with Mak at R.E.I. stealing an ugly shirt simply because it was expensive. Mak has always been much more of a fighter than me so when I walked out of R.E.I. and security approached me, Mak slammed him on the ground so I could get away. The only problem is I didn't feel like running so we both ended up getting hemmed up. Mak didn't even steal anything and he had my back so I felt pretty shitty afterwards for not even trying to get away.

My mom never really seemed to care that I would steal. She was probably happy because it meant she didn't have to figure out a way to get me clothes. She would even be helpful if someone called saying her child got caught stealing. She would play along even if we used a fake name. One time Jay got caught stealing and used a name my mom had never heard before but she went to pick him up anyway knowing it was one of us. Everybody always considered my mom to be real cool. She seemed so sweet and innocent but she definitely had a darker side. Despite her middle-class upbringing, she got in with the wrong crowds and she did prison time for bank robbery. She was definitely no square.

Me and my cousins used to spend a lot of our time in downtown Seattle. Our search for good places to hit the huss took us all over downtown from SoDo, where the Kingdome was, to the Seattle Center, and everywhere in between. We would try to stick to the "ride free area" where buses are free but it was never an issue to simply jump off without paying if we needed to. Besides, it's not like the bus driver was going to get off and chase us. Heading in to downtown you have to pay when you get on the bus so jumping off without paying wasn't an option. If we didn't have any money, sometimes we would have to take the long walk from the CD to downtown. One thing we knew for sure, we would have money for the bus on the way home.

One of our favorite places to go that we discovered while exploring in Downtown Seattle was the Washington Athletic Club. WAC is an athletic club in downtown Seattle that was obviously for people with a lot of money. At this place you can gain access and even charge clothes and food to your account simply by stating your member number and your name. With us being as slick as we were, we got our hands on a sheet of member numbers and it gave us free reign at WAC. I still remember the main member number we would use. Daniel, you don't know me but if you are reading this, I apologize for all the things we charged to your account! We would always go to WAC to get something to eat and play basketball for the most part but sometimes we would buy some shorts or T-Shirts and charge it to a random person's account.

Toward the end of 1995, sports were huge in Seattle. On the heels of Ken Griffey Jr., Randy Johnson, and Edgar Martinez, the Mariners had made an amazing run and made the playoffs, saving baseball in Seattle. We went to the Kingdome quite often during Mariners games to hit the huss outside. Every now and then we would either get tickets given to us by random people outside or somehow work our way in the building so that we could hit the huss in the smoking section.

The Sonics, who were one of the best and most exciting teams in the NBA during the mid-90s, led by Gary Payton and Shawn Kemp, were just about to begin one of the best seasons in franchise history. We knew there would be a lot of people at the game so me and Jay decided to go to the newly renovated Key Arena to hit the huss at the Sonics home opener.

3
THE SONICS

Our favorite way to get from the heart of downtown at Westlake, to the Seattle Center, was the Monorail. Most of the time we would just sneak on. I made it a habit to buy a pretzel with nacho cheese whenever we were on the top floor of Westlake about to ride the Monorail. If I didn't get a pretzel before we got on I would always grab some pizza from Pizza Haven in the Center House immediately when we got off. Our routine for the most part was usually the same.

We were there long before the game but there were Sonics fans everywhere. The city was really buzzing at this time. First, we hit the huss and tried to make a few dollars inside the Center House before walking to Key Arena.

There were ticket scalpers trying to buy and sell tickets every step of the way once we got to the arena. I couldn't get enough of the atmosphere. I had never been inside this building but I wanted to go inside so bad. I was a huge Sonics fan but I had only been to one Sonics game prior. The game I went to was in Portland at the Memorial Colosseum vs the Blazers. My dad got tickets from a friend of his and gave them to me and Fred. I was already a Sonics fan but I became hooked after I was there to see my favorite player Gary Payton hit the game winning shot at the buzzer.

After making a little bit of money we were walking around outside the arena and we discovered the player's parking lot. We stood there and watched several players drive in and get out of their Range Rovers and Land Cruisers before we decided to stand above the staircase they had to walk down to enter the arena. While standing there looking through the metal bars we saw a burgundy Cadillac Deville pull up. We couldn't believe our eyes when the Reign Man, Shawn Kemp, hopped out.

Shawn Kemp was almost everybody in Seattle's favorite player and he had created a huge national following. He had played in three consecutive NBA all-star games by this time and was the most exciting young player in the league. When he approached the staircase we yelled out to him...

"What's up Shawn?", I asked excitedly.

"Yo, Shawn!", Jay yelled.

Shawn Kemp stopped and looked up at us.

"What's goin on fellas?", Shawn asked. "You going to the game?"

"I wish man, we don't have tickets.", I told him.

Shawn Kemp reached in the inside pocket of his leather jacket and grabbed two tickets. He stood on his tippy toes and reach up toward us, tickets in hand and Jay reached down to grab them. We were so excited and could not thank him enough.

"You guys have a good time.", Shawn smiled at us and walked down the stairs to go to work.

When Jay handed me my ticket I looked down and couldn't believe it. These tickets were in the 100 level. Not only were they in the 100 level but they were in the third row! Then again, what else would you expect from the star of the team? We were so excited and extremely grateful. I felt like the luckiest kid in the world. For a short while I was able to forget about the fact that I was a poor kid from the ghetto.

Lines were already super long at the entrance and the doors had not quite opened yet. We hopped in the line and waited until it was our turn to have our tickets scanned for entry. On the way in we made sure to grab a copy of the Sonics Play Ball game day program.

I was amazed by the newly renovated arena. They had video games on the concourse and everything looked so new and clean. We walked into the first aisle we saw although our seats were not there, just to get a quick look at the court. The Sonics had a new logo and new jerseys this year so it was all so fresh and exciting.

We made our way to our seats and the usher made sure to check our tickets. As more and more people came and I noticed that only certain ones were forced to prove they belong where they sat. The seats we were in were very expensive so I probably wouldn't have expected two young kids to be sitting there either.

We were sitting, watching players shoot around when Shawn Kemp came out to get some shots up. When he got out onto the court he looked our way and saluted us. We saluted him back. I couldn't believe that this was real life.

The Sonics had been a good team previously but this year there was a special vibe around the team. I felt like I was watching a very special team. Me and Jay had the time of our life and the Sonics won the game. This was the beginning of one of the most amazing periods of my life.

After meeting Shawn Kemp and getting tickets from him me and Jay decided we were going to come back every time there was a Sonics game. We began to converse with more and more players and before we knew it we had several players who knew us by name and they would give us tickets whenever they could. Even the Sonics television play-by-play guy Kevin Calabro would hook us up from time to time with cards that were good for a free large pizza.

Sometimes players would have family members come in to town or have someone who they had to give their tickets to so they wouldn't have any on them. However, they began to look out for us so much that they would start searching, asking other teammates and having someone leave tickets at will-call for us. Eventually we started asking David Wingate for tickets and he became our most reliable source.

After a while, just getting into the games wasn't enough for us. We decided that after the games we didn't want to leave, we wanted to go back in the locker room area and get autographs. We asked David Wingate to give us the passes that players family members had to get them access after the game and he did. He told us to approach the security guard at the tunnel after the game and tell him that David Wingate had family passes for us. After he did this for us once, it became an all-the-time thing. Sometimes it would be difficult for us to reach him through security because he left too fast or maybe he was having a bad day and said "not today", so we got to know other people who could get us back there. We befriended the wives of players such as Deshawn, the wife of Eric Snow, and she began to give us the passes when David Wingate couldn't. Sometimes if we couldn't get passes we would find ways to sneak in.

We would usually wait right outside of the opposing team's locker room to get autographs and ask for shoes and other memorabilia. The Sonics had to walk this way to get out to their cars so we were able to them and get autographs from them too. I got game worn shoes from almost every player on the team. I was given shoes by Gary Payton, David Wingate, Hersey Hawkins, Detlef Schrempf, Ervin Johnson, Sam Perkins, Vincent Askew, Eric Snow, Steve Scheffler, and more.

We got to know the players on the team. They all had very different personalities. Steve Scheffler was a very funny character. Toward the end of games the crowd would chant his name trying to get him some playing time as the last man off the bench. The crowd would go wild when he would finally be put in by head coach George Karl. The thing I remember most about Scheffler is that if you wanted his autograph you had to answer a trivia question first and, much like Seahawks star Russell Wilson, he always signed his autograph with a bible verse.

I was so poor that I would normally sell the autographed, game worn, shoes to card shops or to this guy named Big Lo, who eventually went on to be known as Seattle's biggest sports fan. This is one of the very few regrets I have. When Gary Payton got elected to the Hall of Fame I instantly thought about how I took his game worn shoes, that it took me months to talk him out of, and sold them to a man who owned a card shop near Key Arena for $200. Gary Payton was an Olympian and an NBA All-Star who won defensive player of the year that year and went to the NBA Finals. Those shoes were worth so much more than what I was given. Today, now that he is in the Hall of Fame, they would be worth even more. I was a poor kid and I was taken advantage of by a grown man.

I became obsessed with getting autographs. Me and Jay started going to the hotels that opposing players stayed at. We were always downtown anyway so it wasn't hard to figure out where they were. We met an extremely young Kevin Garnett in the lobby at the Crowne Plaza. We met a 17-year-old Kobe Bryant while walking around downtown. We once followed Penny Hardaway and Nick Anderson from their hotel to Nike Town. I had a huge collection of cards signed by hundreds of NBA players that I got autographed myself and I wish I still had them today to pass on to my boys.

My most memorable experiences involving opposing team players were with two of the best and most famous NBA players of all-time. The second most memorable came during the 1996 NBA Finals when the Chicago Bulls were in town to play the Sonics. It was me and Jay like always when it came to this type of stuff. We were downtown at the Four Seasons hotel where the Bulls were staying. It was the night before one of the three games played in Seattle during this series.

The NBA Finals and the 72-10 Bulls, the greatest team in NBA history, attracted a big crowd to the Four Seasons. There were quite a bit of people standing together outside the hotel. Of course, me and Jay didn't just stay outside, we went in. We ended up riding in an elevator with Bulls center Bill Wennington and seeing Dennis Rodman, John Sally and a few other Bulls players before getting kicked out of the hotel. When we got kicked out, Michael Jordan was being escorted out by security guards right behind us. Security did not allow anyone to get near Michael and they made it clear he would not be signing autographs. I told them I didn't care and I was going to follow them until Michael signed my card. I followed them and Michael Jordan, the greatest athlete in the history of the world, turned to me and asked "Shouldn't you be at home in bed?" I told him that I was there to see him and continued following. I followed them all the way from the Four Seasons to a restaurant called "The Brooklyn", where Jordan met up with analyst Ahmad Rashaad, who is from Tacoma, for dinner.

When they went inside to eat I walked back to the four seasons. When I got back a newscaster said he saw me talking to Michael Jordan as we were walking away and asked what he said to me. After I told him of our exchange the newscaster asked if I wanted to be interviewed for the nighttime news. I agreed and I was asked maybe 5-10 questions on camera. A short while after filming I was invited into the news truck to watch. Despite all the questions I was asked, they only showed me answering one question on the news…

"What were you thinking when you saw Michael Jordan?" the interviewer asked.

"He was tall.", I said, not knowing what else to say.

That was it. I said he was tall and that was the end of my segment. I was still happy to be on the news and a lot of people asked me about it the next day.

My most memorable experience involving opposing players came one time when the Phoenix Suns came into Seattle. Me and Jay were downtown hitting the huss when we saw what looked like a team bus going by. We knew the Suns were coming in to town because we paid close attention to the schedule. We decided to chase the bus and we knew it would be easy since the downtown streets were so crowded. We followed the bus until it came to a stop at the Sheraton hotel.

We stood and watched the Phoenix Suns get off of the bus until finally, the star of the team, Charles Barkley got off. Me and Jay were just standing there catching our breath and Charles walked up to us and said "Y'all are crazy running after us like that, what's your names?" He must have been watching us out of the tinted bus windows.

We told him our names and he asked what we were doing there instead of being at school and we made some lame excuse when we really were just skipping. He asked us to wait for him outside and said he would be back. We waited out there for about 20 minutes, not knowing why he wanted us to wait. When he finally came back out he was with assistant coach Donnie Nelson, son of famous head coach Don Nelson, and Donnie Nelson's wife. Charles asked me and Jay if we wanted to come with them to eat and we were ecstatic so of course we said yes.

Charles asked us about ourselves while we walked a short distance to the Palomino Italian restaurant at City Center. My heart was racing as we headed up the escalator, I couldn't believe we were actually there with Charles Barkley. We were seated at our table and handed menus and the whole experience was unreal to me.

I was surprised to see that Charles was a professional athlete who didn't eat vegetables. I can't remember what he ordered but he made sure it had no veggies. Me and Jay ordered some type of pasta but when our food came we didn't like it. We had no problem telling Charles that the food was gross and he called over a server. Charles told the server that we didn't like our food and they asked what they could do for us to accommodate. We told them nothing on the menu sounded good and the server said that she would have the chef make us pizza which was not even on the menu. This was a pretty high-class restaurant and not only would we have never eaten there if we were not being treated by Sir Charles, but we damn sure would not have been able to eat food that isn't even on the menu. We ate the Pizza and had a nice little conversation before Charles paid the bill, despite Donnie's objections, and we went our separate ways.

This was a once in a lifetime experience. Later we got taken out to eat at a small restaurant in the CD called Helens by Eric Snow, with Gary Payton a table away. However, we had already had many interactions with them so it wasn't as special. We ran into Eric Snow across the street from Helens at a barbershop called Earl's where alot of the Sonics got their hair cut. We were grateful but it was no big deal for us because we had even rode in his Range Rover before.

Charles Barkley on the other hand was an MVP and Olympian with commercials on national television. He took two poor kids he had never seen before along with him for an unforgettable experience. This is something that he will never get any credit for and I never really hear anything positive said about him, but I can't imagine many other superstars of his status doing this.

It wasn't long before we saw Charles again. We never told him about our connections with the Sonics but after the Sonics beat the Suns the next night, there we were standing outside the Suns' locker room trying to get autographs. I asked Charles to sign my card and I couldn't believe it when he said no. He had a contract that only allowed him to sign a certain brand. I wondered if maybe he felt like he wasted the experience he had given us since we not only were at the game, but on top of that had access to the locker room area. I'm not too sure what he was thinking when he saw us but he truly did give two under-privileged kids one of the most memorable experiences of their childhood.

Outside of the countless amazing experiences at the Key on game day, I had a few other really amazing experiences involving Sonics basketball. There was this new state-of-the-art video game arcade that opened in downtown Seattle and the Sonics had a party there. Of course, although we were not invited, we heard about it and showed up. Gameworks was closed to the public early that day and the party was exclusively for the Sonics players and staff along with their family and friends.

When we got there, we told the security that we were David Wingate's nephews but they wouldn't let us in or make an attempt to track Wingate down. We knew if only one of the players saw us they would let us in but that was impossible from outside. We were too resourceful to be denied so we walked around to the other side where they had two exit doors. It took a little while but eventually someone came out the exit door and we crept right in.

This wasn't my first time inside of Gameworks but I was still super excited to be there for a Sonics party. It wasn't long before we started bumping into players and got our hands on some of the unlimited game cards that were given to everyone. My favorite game to play was Pop-A-Shot so I rushed straight to it. After that I played a little bit of everything.

Eventually, the party was about to end and it was almost time for the last bus so we hurried out and tried to make it to the bus stop so we wouldn't be stranded. This wasn't the first time that we got there too late and were forced to decide between taking the long walk home or walking around downtown taking frequent stops inside of hotels like the Four Seasons, the Sheraton, or the Westin to stay warm until the first bus in the morning. If we stayed downtown, we would only have to kill four hours before buses start running again. On this night, we chose to stay downtown.

We were walking past the Westlake Mall on the back side when a two-door Porsche rolled up beside us, stopped, and the window rolled down. Jay immediately got out of sight and hid. I just stood there.

"What the fuck are you doin out here boy?", a voice strongly yelled out of the window.

I didn't say anything. It was dark and I couldn't see who it was so I walked up to the car. Inside I see Gary Payton staring back at me with the angriest look on his face. I didn't recognize the person who was in the driver's seat.

"Get that big ass fro over here, how you gonna hide wit that fro!", Gary yelled out to Jay. It was obvious now how he recognized us. Jay had this outrageously big afro, it was hard to miss.

"It's just GP come on." I said as I signaled Jay to come to the car.

We stood there and got lectured about being out in the streets in the middle of the night before we convinced Gary that we were just leaving the party and on our way to the bus stop and he drove off. It's too bad they were in a two-seater because we really could have used a ride home.

The only Sonics player who ever took the time to give us a ride home after a game was David Wingate. I really appreciated all of those guys but David Wingate went above and beyond to try to get us inside of every game and even gave us money out of his pocket. He used to tell us we were going to have to come to his house to wash his car in return but we never did. I remember Eric Snow once wanted us to show our gratitude by bringing him gummy bears, that we actually did do.

Another really cool experience I had was at the Key, after a Sonics game had ended. All of the fans had exited the building and we had been back in the locker room area getting autographs and trying to collect shoes and doing what we do. There was a ball rack sitting right outside the Sonics locker room door so me and Jay both grabbed a ball and went out on the Key Arena floor to shoot around. This was a big deal for us because this is floor the Sonics played on. After a while, Sonics head coach George Karl's son, future NBA player Coby Karl, and one of his friends, joined us to shoot around. A couple players were standing around having a conversation and eventually a couple more walked up.

After shooting for a little while we decided to play two-on-two. I'll be honest we completely underestimated these guys. In front of several Sonics players and many other people me and Jay got our asses kicked 11-1. I scored the only point for us and I bragged and bragged about that for the longest because Jay didn't score and I did. This was a very memorable experience for me even though we lost because I was on the Sonics floor playing in front of some of the Sonics.

I would say the most memorable experience I had at Key Arena was game seven of the 1996 Western Conference Finals against the Utah Jazz. Really, that whole series was an amazing experience. The building was jumping, there was never an empty seat. The whole city was buzzing.

The Sonics beat the Jazz to advance to the NBA Finals and I was right there by the court. When the final buzzer sounded, I climbed over to the courtside section and stood on the court watching the celebration. The players were hugging and celebrating, more and more people were crowding around, the fans were blowing the roof off the building, it was insane.

I never had another experience like this. I attended the 2013 NFC Championship game between the Seattle Seahawks and San Francisco 49ers when the Seahawks advanced to Super Bowl 48 after Richard Sherman made himself the most famous football player around with "The Tip", but the major difference for me is that with the Sonics I was right there on the court as opposed to far away from the field and I actually felt like I was a part of the Sonics family.

I remember prior to game 7, a lot of the Jazz players were telling me I couldn't have their shoes because they needed them. After game seven I managed to get them from a couple players. I was talking to Jazz center Greg Foster and he agreed to give me his shoes right before Jay walked up and asked for them too. He ended up giving us both one shoe. I also got game shoes from Antoine Carr and Howard Eisley. I asked Hall of Fame point guard and Gonzaga alum John Stockton for his shoes and his response was "Why would I give you my shoes?" I already didn't like him or Karl Malone because of the battles against the Sonics but after that I really didn't like him.

Once the Sonics made it to the Finals, tickets all of a sudden weren't so easy to get from players any more. The reasons why are pretty obvious. The NBA Finals against Michael Jordan is sure to bring out plenty family members and friends. We obviously didn't have the money to buy tickets, the prices were sky high. We had to resort to sneaking in. Sometimes it would take a while but we always found a way. When we didn't have tickets, we would constantly be on the move because whenever we would find empty seats either the ticket holder would come or an usher would kick us out.

The Sonics ended up losing that series and that is the closest they would ever come to a championship during my lifetime. I wasn't born yet in 1979 when they won the title. After a couple years of having access to the team, players like David Wingate and Eric Snow left and we stopped going around as much.

4
THE PUBLIC SCHOOL SYSTEM

Growing up I attended 15 different schools. Keep in mind that there are only 12 grades plus kindergarten. I dropped out permanently in what should have been the 11th grade. I have gone to schools in many different districts and several different cities including Seattle, Burien, Tacoma, Vancouver, and Portland.

In school I was always in trouble. Whether it was elementary school, middle school, or high school it seems like I just couldn't stay on task. Although I was always in trouble I was always one of the smarter kids in class, if not the smartest. I credit my dad for passing me his genes as well as many things to read. I was able to read at a level many grades ahead of where I was supposed to be at throughout my childhood.

When I first started middle school, my family lived in the south end of Seattle in a neighborhood called Columbia City. For some reason, although we lived in the south end, I had to go to McClure Middle school in the Queen Anne neighborhood. I remember long rides on the school bus. Luckily the driver always played my favorite radio station, Kube 93, so we could listen to music on the way there.

In the beginning, things were going good for me at McClure. I was doing well in my classes and I was excited for the chance to play basketball for my school. I went to school every single day at the start of the year and I was focused on my work. There was an obvious improvement from the previous year in 5th grade. One of the main reasons I was doing so good is because I moved out of the CD which meant that I wasn't as close to Jay's house and school. It wasn't as easy to get to him so I for the most part just got on the school bus like I was supposed to.

Although school was going well, life was still pretty much the same. We were still living in poverty, our house was still too small for our family. I still had to make a way out of no way. I would still meet up with my cousins after school to steal clothes and hit the huss.

I can remember the excitement and optimism that I had in regards to the upcoming basketball season at McClure. Previously I had played for Rotary Boys & Girls club but playing for and representing my school was a different level. At the Boys & Girls club you pay the fee and you get a roster spot. However, at school I would have to make the team. Playing basketball with other students in my grade gave me confidence that I would have been one of the better players on the 6th grade team that year.

Sadly, I never got a chance to put on that McClure jersey. My enrollment there was cut short less than two months into the 6th grade. This time I didn't leave the school as a result of my parents' bad habits or as a result of being forced to move. This time there was no other reason for me leaving besides racism and discrimination. I was about to be thrusted down the school-to-prison pipeline.

One day, shortly after I arrived at school, I was pulled into the principal's office.

"Do you know why you got asked to come to my office today?", the principal asked me.

"No, why?", I responded, with a confused look on my face.

I honestly had no idea what I was doing there. I was often a visitor to the principal's office in elementary school but this was my first time as a middle school kid. I was very nervous. I figured that maybe the school has been alerted by the QFC down the street that I had been there stealing candy or something.

"Can you tell me what happened yesterday after school?", he asked.

I had no idea what he was talking about. Nothing had happened after school. I hopped on the bus and went downtown just like any other day.

"Nothing happened after school!", I proclaimed as my nervousness turned to curiosity.

I knew that I hadn't done anything wrong. I knew that I had nothing to worry about. But still, I didn't know what I was doing there.

"Right after school I got on the bus and left.", I said.

"How much money did you take from him?", the principal asked.

"I don't know what you're talking about, what money and from who?", I responded.

"We know what you did. We were told by another student that after school you pushed him down and took his money out of his pocket. We know you did it so it doesn't make sense to lie.", he said.

I was stunned. I couldn't believe what I had just heard. Why in the world would anyone be accusing me of doing something that is so out of character? I was not that type of kid at all to act out violently and I definitely wouldn't commit what is basically strong-armed robbery.

"I did not do that!" I yelled out in disbelief. "Who in the heck said I did that?", I asked?

"It doesn't really matter who. All that matters is that we know you did it. He identified you and his parents confirmed that he came to school with the money.", he said.

"Identified me? What made him think it was me and who said this?", I asked feeling so confused and now somewhat worried despite my innocence.

"No one else has a jacket like yours and although he did not see your face he identified you by your jacket.", the principal said.

Jay had this pullover Sonics Starter jacket that he had gotten autographed by pretty much the whole Sonics team. He had traded me the jacket in exchange for something, what I can't quite remember. I used to wear this jacket every day. The Sonics were extremely popular and this was Seattle so there is no way they could punish me based on a jacket I thought!

"This is a very serious situation. We cannot have our students becoming victims and getting robbed. You are no longer welcome here and you will be expelled from Seattle Public Schools.", the principal said.

I couldn't believe what I was hearing. I basically had no chance to defend myself. It was my word against some white kid and the people making the decisions looked a lot more like him than like me. There was nobody there to have my back. There was nobody fighting on my behalf. If this were a court of law I would have at least had a crappy public defender but here I had no one. I was a child. They told me that my mom could appeal the decision but she was too caught up in her own bad habits and honestly didn't care enough.

I had been suspended before in elementary school for little petty stuff but I had never been in this type of trouble. I couldn't believe that I was not only kicked out of McClure but I was kicked out of all of the schools in the district. The only way that I would have a chance to get back into a normal public school within the Seattle Public School district would be if I could complete a re-entry program. Re-entry programs are where they send the worst of the worse problem causing kids within the district.

There were no alternative middle schools in the district so I was sent to a middle school re-entry program at an alternative high school called Marshall. In my opinion, it would be very devastating to the development of any 6th grader to get sent to even a normal high school, so imagine how devastating it is for a 6th grader to get sent to an alternative school for kids who were either kicked out of or didn't fit in with normal public school for various reasons. This is where you would find a lot of the female students who had gotten pregnant or had a baby, you would find a lot of gang members who had gotten expelled for fights or weapons. I was from the hood and I grew up around a lot of gang members and even had them in my family but this still was not a place that I belonged or was even comfortable at. You have to remember that during this same calendar year I was still a 5th grader at Bailey Gatzert elementary. A matter of weeks ago I was in a school for 6th, 7th and 8th graders. Now all of a sudden I am catching the bus to school with people who are 18, 19 and even 20 years old and still seniors in high school.

I showed up at Marshall when I was supposed to. I was still dedicated to school. I was having a great year at McClure and I didn't plan on having that stop just because I got lied on and discriminated against. However, it didn't take me long to realize that this environment was not for me. My very first day there were students talking shit in class and disrespecting the teacher. I could tell this place was not for me. Days later in the gym after lunch I overheard a couple students talking about robbing me after I pulled out my wad from hitting the huss at the vending machine. I didn't feel like this environment had anything to offer me so I walked right out the side door in the gym during PE and never came back. To my knowledge this school never came looking for me. They never fought to get me back in there. They allowed me to become a dropout in the 6th grade.

My mom gets a lot of the blame for me quitting school at such a young age, but she was trapped in her addiction and that disease is debilitating. You would think that a school district would be equipped to at least reach out to a kid who stopped attending. I stayed out of school all through December, January, February, March and most of April that year. Eventually we were on the move again and we moved to Burien which meant I was no longer in the Seattle Public School district and I could return to a normal school.

I started the school year in the 6th grade at McClure Middle School. I was expelled and sent to Marshall Alternative High School. Once I moved to Burien and into a new school district, I was sent to Hazell Valley Elementary School. I am the only person that I know of who was enrolled at a middle school, a high school and an elementary school all in the same year. Imagine the type of psychological impacts that would have. Could you picture yourself in my shoes? I finished the year going to recess!

The whole 6th grade was basically a huge gap for me academically. Somehow, the way these public schools are set up, I still completed the 6th grade after attending Hazell Valley to finish the year. I began the 7th grade in the same district at Sylvester Middle School.

I really liked Sylvester a lot. Once again I was one of the better basketball players in my grade. I just knew I was going to make the team. Me and all my friends were super excited about the upcoming tryouts. Like always, something had to go wrong and I never ended up playing basketball there.

Shortly after school started we ended up losing our apartment in Burien. My mom ended up going to treatment for her cocaine addiction and my step-dad moved into this clean and sober housing unit near downtown Seattle called the Aloha Inn. I remember living with my sister Nikki and visiting Fred at the Aloha Inn and visiting my mom at the treatment center. After a while, my mom's inpatient treatment was complete and she moved into a small apartment in Tacoma where me, Yakini and Sareeta moved with her.

While I lived with Nikki, who lived in the Seattle Public School district, I was forced to go back to an alternative high school for the re-entry program. This time I ended up at Sharples. Sharples always had a reputation for being for the baddest of the bad kids, at least that's what I had heard. Although I was enrolled, I never used to go. I never had any consequences for this and no one came looking so it didn't matter, right? Once we moved to Tacoma with our mom I was sent back to a normal middle school within the Tacoma Public School district.

At Jason Lee I began to actually like school again. I was in Tacoma then so I was away from my cousins and meeting with them every day in downtown Seattle was over with. I didn't know my way around Tacoma and my cousins weren't coming out there. I began to see them less and less and coincidentally I began getting in less trouble at school. My favorite part of going to Jason Lee was the glassblowing class which was something that no Seattle school had. We were introduced to the work of Tacoma native Dale Chihuly and we were allowed to utilize the glass blowing lab to create our own glass art. I created vases, cups and paperweights and I would always come home so proud of my creations that I could give to my mom.

It was not long before my mom and my step-dad were both able to find jobs and rent us a big house to live in that could fit all of our family comfortably for the first time in a long while. They were both clean and sober and things were looking up for us. Going to treatment was a great thing for my mom. We were actually a real family. We ate meals together and spent pretty much every day together. I was no longer out running the streets like kids my age had no business doing. I was being raised properly and taken care of.

At the beginning of the 8th grade my mom had taken me and my sisters to the Super Mall to go school shopping and given us all a bunch of money to pick out our own stuff. We had come a long way from when I would have to provide for myself if I wanted nice things. This was the same year that we got our first computer. I used to spend all day every day on that thing. This also ended up being my best year ever in school and we also had our best Christmas ever this year. Life was great.

When basketball tryouts came around that 8th grade year I was still a student at Stewart Middle School. I actually got to try out for the team, made the team and got to play the full season! This was the best year ever. I got in some minor trouble at school but nothing too serious. I got suspended one time for going to Jack in the Box during lunch instead of eating at school and I got suspended on the last day of school for calling my teacher Mrs. Albert, "Mr. Albert." I passed all of my classes but I was still suffering the consequences of the gaps in my education from previous years. I was horrible with math because there was so much I was not present to learn. I didn't know how to do multiplication and division on paper but I could do it in my head. I would often get deducted points even when I had the right answer because my process was not the same as the one they were trying to program into us. I had trouble showing my work and this costed me. Fortunately, I had a D in pre-algebra and that was enough to get me into high school.

Over the summer in between the 8th and 9th grade I spent all of my time on the computer. I was extremely fascinated by the internet. There were so many different things I could do. I figured out how to download movies, music and video games. I taught myself how to build websites. I learned a lot of HTML, PHP and CGI coding. I downloaded a lot of very expensive software like Photoshop and Dreamweaver and I taught myself how to use them.

One of the things that I used to do on the computer back then is this thing called an E-Fed. E-Fed stands for E-Federation. A bunch of kids would create websites and recruit people to take on the role of a professional wrestler. Some E-Feds would be limited to using real wrestlers while other's let you create your own persona. Participants would use online message boards to write out these extravagant role-playing scripts attempting to better their opponent. Whoever created the best scripts throughout the week would usually end up winning the simulated wrestling match. This was all text based. A lot of people out there are probably great writers today because of participation in E-Feds in their youth.

When the 9th grade started, I was ready to continue with the good work from the previous year. I was enrolled at Lincoln High School and we surprisingly still lived in the same house as the previous year. High school was a different ballgame than middle school and I ended up having issues with attendance and being off-task. I went to basketball tryouts that year but I skipped a couple of the morning sessions so I never even went to see if I made the team. Those morning tryouts were mandatory so I didn't think I could make the team without attending them all and a couple friends of mine used to joke and tell me the coach put a band-aid over my name, meaning I got cut. It's too bad because being a part of that team might have kept me in school. Several friends of mine went on to be part of the varsity teams that were the first in the history of Tacoma to win back-to-back state championships.

Before the end of the 9th grade I ended up dropping out again. I had an afro and I allowed my sister to put a perm in my hair because she said it would be easier to braid that way. After putting the perm in my hair, my hair was ruined. My hair was so straight that it couldn't hold braids so I was stuck looking like an old school pimp. I refused to go to school because I knew that people would crack jokes at my expense. I never went back to Lincoln and I hardly earned any high school credits that year.

The next year I was enrolled at Oakland Alternative High School. Although I had bad experiences with alternative schools before I decided to give Oakland a chance. I went for about a week but I was not feeling it so I once again became a drop-out. Eventually, in what would have been my 10th grade year, we moved back to Seattle. I was enrolled in yet another alternative school that I went to a couple times before stopping. I hardly attended class at all that whole year. In the 11th grade the same thing happened again. I was enrolled at Southlake Alternative and I was in the same class as my cousin Mak. However, neither one of us lasted long there. That was the last school I ever went to. I was tired of being in alternative schools so I gave up on ever graduating. I was done with school for good so I dropped out at the age of 16.

5

ELEVATED THE HUSTLE

I had a job in 2001. It was at a sports store called The Sports Warehouse right across the street from where the Mariners and Seahawks both play. I was one of probably 10 members of my family who worked there at some point. Even Jay worked there.

The Mariners of 2001 were one of the best teams in baseball history winning a record-tying 116 games. Every single game was packed with fans and probably about half of these fans would have to pass by one of the two Sports Warehouse stores making their way to Safeco Field. I spent time that year working at both stores and I also had my own satellite stand. My duties included making cotton candy, helping customers find products, cleaning, or whatever else I was asked to do. The thing I remember most about the satellite stand is selling countless mini American flags after the 9/11 terrorist attacks. I will forever be cognizant of blatant attempts to appeal to the patriotism within the people in order to cash-in. I see it all the time!

I enjoyed working at The Sports Warehouse but I was paid "under the table" in cash. Because I was being paid under the table I made less than minimum wage. Although the money wasn't good, I still had fun interacting with the fans. Every now and then I was given tickets by random fans so I got to go watch some of the game sometimes. I always had to be back at work before the game ended to catch the fans on their way out.

At the end of the Mariners season I was done working there because I knew I could make way more money doing other things. The store didn't stay open much longer after I stopped working there. The owner was killed working concessions at Kube 93.3 Summer Jam at the Gorge. He will always be remembered by my family because so many of us worked for him.

It was only a matter of time before I was done with school permanently. I didn't really feel like I had a chance to graduate and things always went wrong for me when it came to school. I wonder sometimes, had I never been expelled and cast out of Seattle Public Schools, how much different would things have turned out for me? I still moved around a lot, my life was very unstable throughout childhood. So who knows, maybe nothing would have been different.

In early 2002, we had been living at the Highpoint projects in West Seattle and a lot of the people around me started selling crack. When it came to projects and shelters in Seattle I swear it seems like we lived in them all. There are not a lot of people who lived in Yesler Terrace, Rainier Vista, and Highpoint. There are even less people who have lived in the CD, the Southend, the West, Hilltop, the East Side, and Northeast Portland. I have lived in almost every well-known (for the wrong reasons) "Hood" from Seattle to Portland. In these types of environments crack cocaine users and dealers were everywhere.

While my friends and cousins were on the block selling crack, a lot of the time I would be right there with them. I easily could have been doing it myself but I refused to ever touch that shit. There was no way I was about to sell crack to somebody else's mom after everything I had been through in my life as a result of my own mom smoking it. Despite my personal reluctance to make money that way, I didn't knock my friends and cousins for doing what they were doing. I know how it is, we didn't have many options. I knew they were just doing what they had to do and doing what so many people from our background end up doing to put food on the table and clothes on their back.

I never had a problem with drug dealers. My whole life I was surrounded by them. I just refused to be one myself. Well, I did sell weed on Broadway for a little bit. What we knew as $10 bags would easily go for $20 on Broadway. I didn't do it long though, selling drugs just wasn't for me. It's not that I couldn't have been good at it, I just didn't like to do it and I didn't want to play a role in someone's mom's addiction.

Eventually, as time went by, I started hearing and seeing increasingly more people getting involved with schemes involving bad checks. A lot of the same people who had normally seen selling drugs as their only option started to realize that there were ways to make a lot more money in a lot less time. It wasn't long before Mak met this female who worked at a check cashing business and I finally had my opportunity to hit that quick lick.

When Mak met Natalie, I don't think either one of us had ever seen $1,000 at the same time. We had always hustled and made money, but it was more on a petty level, just trying to obtain life's basic necessities. His relationship with her gave us the opportunity to touch more money than we had ever touched before.

When Mak heard that Natalie worked at a check cashing business any attraction he may have had to her was multiplied by 100. Although he was far more interested in getting money he didn't mind having to hang out with her and get to know her a little bit. When I was around them both at the same time he made it extremely clear what he wanted most and he made no attempts to trick her or con her into giving it to him. He would constantly bring up the idea of cashing bad checks and try to get her to agree to do it for him.

After about a month, Mak had finally convinced Natalie to allow me and him both to come in one day and cash a check. She knew her job well, so she didn't have much fear of getting caught. She just wanted to make sure that Mak was happy because she really liked him. She definitely liked him a lot more than he liked her.

When she agreed to cash the checks for us I was nervous, but at the same time, I was excited that I could possibly get my hands on thousands of dollars. We decided on Monday, that come Friday, Mak would go in and cash his check for $2,500 and I would come in shortly after and do the exact same thing. Over the next few days I was trying everything I could to get my hands on a check. There were a lot of people who talked about doing these schemes so it seemed like access to a single check would be automatic. However, when it came time to try to get one, it was outside of my price range. I was not willing to give up half the money in order to get the check.

At that time, my sister's boyfriend, who is the father of her daughter, lived with us. He had opened a checking account and he had a box of checks just sitting around the house. I was very desperate and I wanted this money bad that I did what I had done my whole life and stole. I took a single check out of one of his checkbooks with no remorse because I figured he had nothing to lose. He didn't have enough money in the bank to cover the check and he could easily deny that he wrote it. I didn't know anything about checks or banks at the time but I was pretty sure I wouldn't harm him. He was like a big brother to me and I had love for him so I definitely didn't want to cross him. However, I had in front of me what I believed to be the opportunity of a lifetime and I was going to pursue it. I was misguided and blinded so I didn't recognize how messed up what it was of me to steal his check.

When the day rolled around that we were supposed to go in and cash the check I began to have second thoughts. I started to wonder what would happen if I went inside of there and Natalie wasn't the person at the register. Would I ask for her? That would be suspicious, wouldn't it? I envisioned having the doors locked on me and being trapped until the police came. The thing that gave me the confidence to go through with it was the fact that Mak had to go first and if it didn't work for him, then obviously, I would not be going in there.

I met Mak around the corner from the check cashing business where Natalie worked and we went over our plans. We both filled out our checks, made payable to a fake name of course. I sat nervous as hell as I watched Mak walk away, hoping he would come back with good news. It was about a 4-minute walk from where we met to the check cashing business. I imagined that it couldn't possibly take him more than 15 minutes to get back.

As time went by I got more and more nervous. Eventually over 30 minutes had passed and Mak still hadn't returned. I decided that I was going to walk over by the check cashing business to make sure there were no police there and that he was still inside. I made my way there and I saw no cop cars, everything looked normal, Mak was standing at the counter with Natalie on the other side. I was relieved to see that he was not being arrested but at the same time I didn't understand what was taking so long. I decided to walk back to our meeting spot and wait patiently.

Not even five minutes after I got back, Mak walked in with the biggest smile on his face and gave gestures that made it obvious his check was cashed successfully.

"Did it work? What took so long?" I asked him.

"Hell yeah! We are on for life!" He said.

"Why were you in there so long?"

"There was somethin wrong with the computer but they fixed it.

When you cash a check for the first time you have to give them all kinds of information and shit then they give you a little card. Shit took forever."

"Damn, I thought you got booked. I walked over there and when I saw that you were still in there I was like damn somethin must be wrong!"

"Hell naw it was all gravy, let's just wait like 20 minutes then you can go in there."

We decided we were going to grab something to eat really quick. We had met at a fast food restaurant so it worked out perfectly. I had just enough time to eat and then it would be my turn to commit my first felony. Up to this point I had no reservations about committing a crime in order to get what I needed or even wanted. However, this was taking it to a whole new level. There were so many ways that this could go wrong. We could not only make Natalie lose her job, but she could also go to jail for what she was doing. If she went to jail it would only be a matter of time before she told on us and we were right behind her. Now wasn't the time for doubt. My cousin just walked out with a couple thousand dollars in his pocket and there was no way I was about to pass up that opportunity. The check I was cashing was from an account with insufficient funds so in my mind I wasn't stealing from any specific person. I was going in there with no ID and using a fake name so it couldn't be traced back to me. The inside connection gave me the confidence to go through with it. I was all in at this point.

After we finished eating I walked out the door and walked over to the check cashing business that Natalie manned the counter for. My heart was racing, I was very nervous. However, my excitement and thinking about what I could do with the money by far outweighed any fear I might have had. I walked up to the register, said hello, and handed her the check. I was asked some basic questions that I had memorized the answers to so that I could have an account created and be given the card that Mak had told me about. Good thing it was Natalie at the register because it had to be obvious that I was using made-up information. Within about 10 minutes of me walking in that door Natalie counted out the money and handed me $2,500 minus the check casing fee in an envelope. I smiled, thanked her, and headed to the door.

I could not contain my excitement. This was like an adrenaline rush. I had over $2,000 in my pocket. I felt rich. I felt like anything I wanted could be mine. When I got back to Mak we decided that we had way too much money to be hopping back on the bus, which is how we both got there. Mak decided to called one of his female friends and she came to pick us up. Once we got in the car Mak gave her a $100 bill and told me to do the same so she could drive us around for the day. Reluctantly, I agreed. That was a lot of money for a ride. I wasn't trippin though this was free money in my eyes so I handed her a C note and we went on our way to start spending. We didn't even go visit Natalie afterwards and this became a one-time thing. She was expecting us to take care of her and give her some of the money but we were moving too fast and didn't really have time to go sit up under her. We had money to spend and moves to make.

We went to a couple different malls and bought shoes and clothes. We had to have the latest and greatest. Within a couple of days, I realized I was going to run through this money very fast. I had always assumed that $1,000 was a whole lot of money that could last a long time. I was a little upset with myself for having run through so much money so fast. I didn't want to ever be broke again.

I decided to have my mom hold $1,000 for me so that no matter what I couldn't drop below that amount of money. I took a trip to Portland with Jay, Mak and a couple of friends. I was gone for maybe a week. I ended up spending every dime I took with me to Portland so the money my mom was holding was all I had left. We were staying at an expensive hotel in Portland called the Double Tree and we all had to chip in. I had to buy food and of course we spent money on clothes and shoes at the Mall. Leaving that money with my mom seemed like a great idea at the time because I know I would not have left Portland with $1,000 had I taken all of my money with me.

When I got back from Portland I planned on getting a couple hundred dollars from my mom just so I could have some money in my pocket. However, when I asked her for it, she told me that my money was gone. The story she told me was that her crack dealer told her he could triple it for her within a couple days and she didn't think I would be back before he returned the money to her. The only problem is there never was any drug dealer promising her anything, she had spent my money getting high with my step-dad and her friends.

I was highly upset, I was devastated actually. But what could I do? This was my mom. She didn't have that type of money to pay me back. I would never think about causing any harm to her. I had to just go ahead and take it as a loss. I guess this was my first true lesson that demonstrated the result of chasing fast money. As fast as money comes, is as fast as money goes.

I was back at square one and broke again. I guess you could say I deserved it. I am a strong believer in Karma. Well, my own idea of what Karma is. I believe that taking one of my sister's boyfriends checks and not giving Natalie a cut was for sure to lead to some sort of negative outcome. I screwed a couple different people over in the situation so it's only right that I got screwed over too.

I never cashed another bad check myself like that. I would have if another opportunity came along with an inside connection but it never did. There were a lot of people bold enough to try with no inside connection but I wasn't the one. Eventually, I decided to start trying to get other people to do it for me but it never worked out.

I got involved in a couple small schemes to get paid like I did cashing that check but nothing ever seemed to pan out. After a while, word on the street was that the way to really get big money was to find someone who had a bank account to cash your checks. Apparently, they didn't even need to go in and cash the check because you could deposit the check through the ATM machine without them being present as long as you had their card and pin number. This also meant less risk for them because they could deny everything and report their card stolen. This seemed really complicated to me and I didn't get involved right away but eventually once I saw my older cousins getting paid from it I went out and tried to get a card.

Probably two months had passed since I had cashed the check at Natalie's job and I had finally convinced someone to give me their bank card. I was making small amounts of petty money in between but I was very excited at the possibility of touching thousands again. I immediately contacted Jay right when I got the card and I decided I was going to let him handle it since everything was so complicated. He told me I could either accept half of the money, or I could accept his 1992 white Cadillac Sedan Deville regardless how much was made. He didn't spend a lot of money for the car but that was a hard offer to pass up. I didn't have a driver's license and I had never even drove before but I wanted that car. Besides, things could go wrong with the ATM card that I gave him and the car would still be mine. I gave Jay the card and he gave me the keys to the car.

Shortly after I made this deal with Jay and I got the Cadillac from him, I was riding with Mak, one of our homeboys, and this female Mak was talking to. We stopped at a 7-11 store in the CD and when we got back to the car two dudes ran up on us and told Mak to get out the car. One of the dudes walked up to my door and asked if I got the car off "the lick" and I just ignored him. With how bold these guys were being when there was only two of them and three of us it was more than obvious that they had a gun so we just went along with it as they basically car-jacked me. Mak had always been a fighter but I always avoided confrontation so when I noticed that Mak wasn't about to fight there was no way I was about to fight. Had Mak fought I would have had no choice but in this situation, I felt like our lives were on the line. I didn't want to let them take my car but I damn sure didn't want to get shot. Come to find out these were Natalie's brothers and they were pissed off that we had her cash checks for us. They were even more pissed off that we didn't cut her in.

Looking back, I don't really blame them for having their sister's back but that situation could have gotten really ugly. We could have easily decided to take it to another level and get guns and go look for them but that wasn't really who I wanted to be. Eventually I had no choice but to report the car stolen. When I reported it stolen I didn't tell the real story of what happened. I have never been a snitch and I knew better than even thinking about it. Refusing to snitch isn't just about fear of retaliation but it's just against the rules of the streets. I was entrenched in the street life and I followed the rules of that life. My own family wouldn't have had any respect for me if I had snitched. Reporting the car stolen was bad enough because it could get someone a charge but I had to do something because the car was in my name and there is no telling what might happen. After a couple months, I finally got the car back from the police after a woman tried to register the car in her name.

6

BACK TO THE TAC

In late 2002, we moved from our apartment on Delridge and Thistle in West Seattle, back to Tacoma. This time we moved into a shelter on 15th and Yakima. This was a place where families had to share rooms and there were a lot of rules to follow. I absolutely hated being there but I didn't have any other options. We didn't have to stay here long before we moved across to street to what is called the G Street Shelter, but it was actually more like having our own apartment. This place had cold hard floors and never quite felt like home. After a little while staying here we were able to find a tiny two-bedroom apartment not far away. Our new apartment really was just the separated upstairs portion of somebody's house on 17th and Martin Luther King Jr. boulevard, which is in the Hilltop neighborhood.

Hilltop was known as a being a high-crime, high-poverty, Crip neighborhood. Being from Seattle, you really don't hear anything but bad stories. Even when I lived in Tacoma previously anytime Hilltop was mentioned it was usually not in a positive way. I have never joined a gang but a lot of my friends and family are from Folks and every neighborhood I have ever lived in was full of gangs so I wasn't too worried about that aspect. I moved into the neighborhood with low expectations. However, I enjoyed living there and I had a lot of fun during this period of my life.

I wasn't really getting out into the neighborhood and meeting the people around me because I used to spend all my time going to places like the mall to meet girls. My mom never used to mind if I would bring girls home and it became an everyday thing. I don't know what these girls saw in me because I never made any sort of commitment to them. They all used to love my mom because she would constantly crack jokes and have us laughing. Sometime me and one of my friends would bring some girls over, then when they leave, next thing you know a couple more girls are pulling up. Looking back, I feel bad for being that type of guy but I was very young and heavily influenced by the world around me. All of the males around me growing up were pretty much the same way. In my circle if you had true feelings for a female that was a sign of weakness. We listened to a lot of Too $hort and Mac Dre and music heavily influenced my beliefs. My behavior was typical for people who participate in the culture I was a part of.

While I was living on Hilltop I began to get more involved with bank licks. My family was still dirt poor and getting a job wasn't even on my radar. At the beginning, I never deposited checks or withdrew the money myself. I didn't really know the exact process and I didn't have access to checks. Because I didn't know how to hit bank licks myself, every now and then I would give someone else a card from one of the girls I was talking to. The person I gave the card to would keep half the money and I would split the other half with whoever's bank account it was.

Often, the bank lick didn't even work when I gave the cards to other people. At least, that's what I was getting told. A lot of the time it was other people's greed that kept me down. When you are dealing with liars, thieves, and crooks, trusting them to place thousands of dollars in your hand, there is a pretty big chance that you won't be getting every penny that should have come your way.

I was only able to put up with getting bopped for so long before I decided to take more risks. My mom was poor, as I mentioned, and she was having hard times paying bills, so I told her we could give my cousin her bank account to make some quick money. She agreed to do it so I gave him her ATM card and he hit for over $10,000. My cousin decided for some reason that although it was my mom's card, and he got it from me, that he wanted all the money for himself. You must realize this is someone who I love and trust, and someone who loves and trusts me. If he would get over on me, it was time to stop trusting people period when it came to bank licks. I would still trust this man with my life up to this very day, but back then I could not trust him to give me my fair share from the bank lick. At that point, I realized if I really wanted to make big money, I was going to have to get my hands on some checks and start hitting bank licks myself.

I knew a lot of broke people who had bank accounts so it wasn't hard to get my hands on what I needed to hit bank licks. A lot of people get a job once they are old enough to work and even if they aren't saving money, they still need a bank account where they can cash their checks. Half the time the people who would give me their cards had negative account balances.

I knew that a lot of people were just as money hungry as I was so I decided that I would use that to my advantage. If I ever had a need for checks I would offer pretty much anybody a $100 bill for one of their checkbooks. Clearly, the only people who would be willing to do this had no money in the bank. They knew that the checks wouldn't have their handwriting on it so they could easily report them stolen. I'm sure that a lot of people reported them stolen before I even had the chance to use them but it didn't matter.

By the time I was just getting started with bank licks, Mak had already made a killing. He really influenced me after he had a three-day run in which he hit for $50,000 off of one credit union account. I still remember the day he pulled up to my house on Hilltop in a big body S 500 Mercedes-Benz. Driving a Benz at one point was like an untouchable dream for us. We came from the gutter and grew up dirt poor. We were not far removed from stealing clothes from Eddie Bauer and hitting the Huss just to have life's essentials. Seeing my cousin, who came from a similar struggle, pull up in that big body, really inspired me. The problem is, I was inspired to head further in the wrong direction.

I started to make more money after that because I started going after it way harder. Before, I had only been hitting bank licks to get a couple thousand dollars here and there. I was good until I ran through that and the need arose to hit another one. After seeing my big cousin turn into a straight baller I couldn't be left behind, I wanted that feeling. I wanted to always have a lot of money. I wanted a nice car. I wanted to get my own place.

During that time, I had been driving cheap cars, also known as buckets, that I bought from the tow yard auction for between $150-$300. This was a really fun period of my life. It was the last chance for me to have no responsibilities in the world and I was living life on my terms. I definitely wasn't living my life right but based on my distorted perceptions, I was the man. I had all the Jordan's, nice clothes, and money in my pocket. Those things, of course, attracted the girls.

During this period of my life I learned that a lot of females are really no different than males. I met and hung with a lot of girls who told me they had a boyfriend. Girl after girl would completely violate any relationship they claimed to be in. Obliviously they didn't represent all women. I attracted and was attracted to a certain type but they really made it where I never wanted a girlfriend. There was no way I was about to be that dude who calls some female his girlfriend just for her to be messing around with other guys and making a fool out of me. Although a lot of them would be open about it, some would hide it and I would find out from one of their scandalous friends who was trying to get at me behind their homegirl's back. I developed a mentality where I was never going to commit and I rarely hung with the same girl more than a couple times. If we did hang more than a couple times then we probably just weren't messing around like that and were kicking it as friends.

Once I started having thousands of dollars in my pocket I decided that I would need to protect myself. I was always hearing about people close to me getting set up and robbed and I didn't want to get caught slipping. I asked one of my cousins to find me a gun and he gave me this super old fashioned 22 caliber revolver that had an extremely dangerous hair-trigger. I didn't have the gun for long before I learned just how dangerous it was.

One day I was with two of my home girls who I hung with quite a bit, but strictly on a friend tip. One of them knew I had a gun and she asked me if she could shoot it. I told her that she could shoot it but we needed to go out in the woods somewhere because I was not trying to go to jail or hurt anybody. She knew of a good spot so we went there and we both shot the gun one time at a tree.

When we got back to the car we were sitting there talking and I had the gun in my lap. I wanted to shoot the gun again so I decided I was going to shoot it one more time out of the window before we drove off. There were three bullets left in the revolver so all I had to do was pull back the hammer, raise my arm out the window, and pull the trigger. What ended up happening instead was I pulled back the hammer and sat the gun on my lap while we continued talking. Somebody walked by the car and I got nervous so I decided I wasn't going to shoot the gun again and we were just going to leave. I started to lift the gun off my lap. BOOM! There was a loud blast. I didn't immediately realize what had happened.

I began to feel a burning sensation above my left knee. I had just fucking shot myself. I had just fucking shot myself! I yelled out some curse words and opened my door and stepped out the car. My leg was covered in blood. I had on Makaveli brand jeans which had late rapper, actor, and revolutionary, Tupac Shakur's face on them. The bullet had gone right thru the head of the image of Tupac on my jeans. The bullet entered right above my knee and it must have bounced off and left my body at the middle of my kneecap.

I wasn't in a whole lot of pain but I had no idea what to do. My homegirls were in as much shock as I was and they didn't have any idea what to do either. I decided that I was going to drop them off at home and then go see if my mom knew what to do. Although I had a fresh bullet wound in my leg and there was a lot of blood, I dropped one of them off, then the other, and drove back home to 17th and MLK. I would have thought that getting shot in the knee would have felt a lot worse and prevented me from walking but I could drive and walk. Once I got home I had a big flight of stairs to climb and I was able to get to the top. We lived only a couple of blocks from St. Joseph Medical Center so my mom told me I needed to bring the gun in the house and we should walk over to St. Joes hospital so that I could be checked out by a doctor.

Growing up poor and black you don't really learn about the 2nd amendment or the proper way to go about possessing a gun. Besides, as far as I knew it was never legal for a black man to have a gun. The second amendment doesn't seem to apply to black people the same way it does to other ethnicities. Almost everyone I know of that ever possessed a gun was doing so illegally based on either being too young to have a license, being a convicted felon, or for whatever reason not being informed about how to possess a gun legally. I was worried that I might be charged with a crime so I was a little hesitant to even go to the hospital. My mom told me that the wound could get infected and I could possibly get gangrene so I agreed to go to the doctor for treatment.

Once we got to the hospital and I was seen by a doctor I was asked if I had called the police. I reminded them again that I had shot myself and it wouldn't quite make sense for me to call the police on myself. It was an accident. Little did I realize at the time, it was an accident that probably saved me from a drive-by shooting charge at the least and death at the worst. I had no idea about the laws regarding discharging a firearm in public, especially discharging it outside of a vehicle. I am the type of person that believes everything happens for a reason and shooting myself in the leg is not as bad as what could have happened to me that night had someone called the police and reported a young black man with a gun, shooting out of his car. A lot of the time police shoot first and ask questions later when it comes to black people having guns.

You heard the saying "If it doesn't kill you, it can only make you stronger", right? Well, I see that as a great philosophy and I definitely grew stronger because of this situation. My wound was cleaned up and my leg was wrapped. I was provided anti-biotics to prevent infection. Eventually, I was right back in action but with a new-found sense of awareness when it came to gun safety. I immediately got rid of that gun that I had shot myself with. I decided that I didn't want anything to do with guns or shooting.

That threat of robbery was still out there but I decided I would take my chances. I just knew I didn't want to shoot anybody. I hadn't been in a fight since elementary school and I had no desire to hurt people. I was no punk, but I normally avoided conflict. Fighting was a lose-lose proposition. You can't be walking around with a broken hand or a black eye claiming to have won just because you did more damage to the other person. How is that considered a win for anyone? Shooting someone had to be even more of a lose-lose because you either kill them and go to prison for life, or you don't kill them and they come back to kill you. Besides, violence just isn't my thing.

Not long after I shot myself I started to get tired of living with my mom. We lived in such a small space and I was 18 now so I could finally rent my own place. I was making more than enough money but it took more than money to rent an apartment. You had to actually have a job and proof of income. You had to go through credit checks and things like that. For the time being I was stuck.

It was around this time that met my best friend to this day, Mo. He was a nationally ranked high school basketball player who had moved around quite a bit during his life. He had spent time in Tacoma, multiple cities in northern and southern California, as well as Arizona. It's hard to maintain your national ranking and stay on the radar of colleges when you don't have stability in your life but he kept his name out there. I remember going to his house for the first time and he showed me pictures of him with very famous college basketball coaches. Some of these pictures were even taken at his house. He had a ton of letters from every college you could imagine expressing their interest in him coming to their school to play basketball. He was going to Lincoln, the school I went to in the 9th grade, and he was supposed to help them win their 3rd straight state basketball championship. It was his senior year and since we were both supposed to be part of the '03 graduating class we had some mutual friends from my freshman year.

The thing that led to me and Mo clicking was that fact that we both liked to kick it with girls and have fun. Neither one of us drank liquor or smoked weed. We both loved basketball. I used to pick him up in one of my buckets and we would do our thing. I always thought girls were attracted to flashy things more than anything but although Mo didn't have those things he was a 6'9" athlete and it didn't matter what we were rolling in.

Eventually I had gotten an immaculate 1994 Cadillac Sedan Deville from Jay and the days of riding in buckets were over. This was the first car I owned that I would say was really a nice car. It was extremely clean both inside and out. Although it wasn't brand new or even close, it was still new to me and a benefit of making more money. Bank licks were my every day goal at this point because getting that Cadillac still wasn't the same as Mak buying an S 500.

Shortly after I got my nice car I was able to move into my own apartment. I had met someone who created pay stubs for me to make it look like I had a regular income and this eliminated my only barrier. I found a one bedroom apartment in the Steilacoom neighborhood at the Morning Tree Park Apartments. When I moved in it was late 2003 and my rent was only $445.

I didn't know it at the time but my life was about to change. Although I was breaking the law I was on the verge of trading in a life of poverty for my distorted idea of the good life. Money was no longer an issue for me. I could buy pretty much anything I wanted or needed. I thought that I was getting a lot of girls living on Hilltop but having my own place and hanging with Mo everyday took it to a whole new level.

I didn't really care about the fact that I was living a life of crime that was headed nowhere. After a lifetime of poverty and struggling, the little bit of so-called success I had hitting bank licks completely distorted my perceptions in terms of right and wrong. In my mind, I was helping people far more than I was hurting people. I didn't feel like I was hurting any individuals at all. I told myself the banks were insured so they weren't even taking a loss. Who cares if that was completely made up and just a guess, it allowed me to go about my business with a clear conscience. All the people I was getting ATM cards from and buying checks from decided to break the law to make money just as I did so I didn't look at any of them as victims. They all knew what they were doing just as much as I did, they were no different than I was.

7
BALLIN' OUT

Living in my own place changed my life a lot. For one, I now had the responsibility of being grown, caring for my home, and making sure all the bills got paid. I also could come and go as I wanted without having anyone in my business. I ate a lot of fast food and missed my mom's cooking but that wasn't much to sacrifice compared to being free from the restrictions of living in my mom's two-bedroom apartment.

Having my own place, a nice car, and making good money kept the girls coming. Now, they were more mature and had more of a sense of self-respect unlike the type of girls I would bring home on Hilltop. I guess you could say I raised my standards. I know there are people out there who see things like what I just wrote and take it as disrespect for all women but to be honest if that's how you want to misinterpret what I said then that's your personal problem. There was an obvious difference in the types of females I attracted when I was driving buckets and living with my mom compared to when I was better off with my own place and driving a nice car. For example, many of the females I associated with once I had my own place had a job and their own money. They didn't have boyfriends that they were cheating on.

I had a lot of different females who I talked to and hung out with but I was still anti-commitment. Several different females wanted to be in a relationship with me but that just didn't make sense with how I was living. I liked to be able to just do my thing and not have to worry about how anybody else felt about it. When you are a young black male from the ghetto, who never had positive male role models, your values when it comes to women are all messed up until you have enough experiences that lead to growth. I wasn't this way because I was a bad guy. I was a product of my personal life experiences and influences.

By summer 2004 the money was coming in large amounts. After a while I had stacked up $20,000 which was the most money I had up until that point. I still hadn't touched the type of money that allowed Mak to hop in that S 500 but my Cadillac Deville wasn't enough for me anymore. I was driving around like I always did when I passed a car dealership that caught my eye. It was a small repair shop that also sold cars and that was attractive to me because I figured if I bought a car and anything went wrong they would fix it.

The car that really caught my attention was a black 1996 Lexus LS 400. This car was beautiful. I always wanted a black car with black leather interior and this was my chance. The owner of the dealership gave me the keys and once I took it for a test drive I just had to have it. I traded in my Sedan DeVille and paid him $15,000 cash and it was mine! The first place I drove in my new toy was to the Tacoma Mall to buy some 20-inch chrome rims from Hard Knock Wheels. Unfortunately, the rims I wanted weren't kept in stock so I had to wait for them to get shipped.

I felt like a brand-new man in this car. I really couldn't believe I had just bought a Lexus. I felt like I had finally made it. I was a part of the ballers club now. I didn't even pay attention to the fact that buying this car and the rims left me broke. I knew I could make the money right back. I had ATM cards and checks in my possession and after a couple days I knew I could get right back on.

Shortly after I left the mall I went to a U.S. Bank ATM machine to make a deposit in a bank account I was working at the time. Right when I was done at the ATM two females walked by and I was feeling myself because I just bought a Lexus so I made sure to talk to them and let them know. I asked them if they wanted to come to my place to hang out and they said yes so I went to pick up Mo and we drove to my house.

After we hung out for a little while Mo asked one of them to go in my room with him. She agreed so me and the other young lady, whose name is Theresa, stayed in the living room and talked while they were in my room. It seemed to me like her friend was a little jealous of her because she said a couple things to put her on blast. For example, out of the blue she brought up the fact that she had a baby. When she brought it up, it was not meant to be a good thing. A lot of guys lose interest once they hear stuff like that and I felt like that was her so-called friend's goal, to make me lose interest. I didn't lose interest, besides, all I really wanted was a bank card anyway. I had the same agenda with her that I did with all the other pretty girls I brought home with me.

Eventually, her friend made up a reason to be mad and they both walked out of my apartment in the middle of the night with no buses running and no way to get home. I thought it was funny more than anything but I wasn't going to leave them out there in the middle of the night. I pulled up on them in my car and told them I would drop them off at home. They got in the car and I took them home. I had gotten Theresa's number but like most females I met, I wasn't using it much.

Once my rims came I wanted to be seen as much as possible. You could find me at every major function from Seattle to Tacoma with my boy Mo. We would pull up with the windows down and the music blasting. I went out most days of the week. Back then it seemed like there was always something going on.

Mo had attended an all-boys prep-school in Maine when he was done at Lincoln. When he got back from Maine we linked right up and were pretty much inseparable from there. He had a really good basketball season against some great competition so he had entered his name in the 2004 NBA draft. He wasn't invited to the combine but he had a pre-draft workout set up with the Sonics and I was willing to do anything I could to help him succeed. I tried to make sure that he didn't have any needs that could lead him astray so if there was anything I could do for him I would. I didn't want him getting involved with my illegal activities because he had the opportunity of a lifetime in front of him and if he reached his goals money would be no object. Since I was his boy I knew if he made it that meant I would have made it to. He would have hired me as his business manager at least.

I was still hanging with Mak and Jay regularly, plus Mak's older brother Mega had just gotten out the Feds after a long bid for pimping. These three plus Mo made up the circle of people I was closest to at that time. I had other family who I was close to, and I also had other friends, but on most days, you would find me with these guys.

Sometimes we would get bored staying local and decide to take a trip out of town. We would go to Portland quite a bit. One time I drove all the way to Los Angeles with Mo and Jay and we stopped to see some of Mo's people in Fresno. It seemed like no matter where we were or no matter where we went, Mo always had a connection or knew somebody there. We never had to wait in lines when we would go to clubs. We were always getting something for free.

Los Angeles was a fun trip, I finally had a chance to eat at Roscoe's Chicken & Waffles. I got to walk around in Hollywood where our hotel was. We ran into multiple celebrities out there. One of the highlights was when Mark Curry from one of my favorite TV shows as a kid, Hanging with Mr. Cooper, tried to help us get some girls to come back to our room. He told them we were his nephews but they weren't going for it. We also ran into Nick Cannon and Katt Williams outside of a comedy club on Sunset boulevard.

When I came home from California I immediately got back on my grind and tried making back all the money I had spent on my trip. Before long I had $10,000 sitting in an old shoe in my closet. I went out to one of the 18 and up nightclubs in Seattle and I came home to find that my apartment had been broken into and ransacked. The Morning Tree Park Apartments was not the best apartment community to live in but I never imagined that I would be violated in such a way when my apartment was right across from the office. I figured it had to be someone I knew that got me. It could have been a neighbor but I don't know if a neighbor would have risked me coming home while they were in my apartment. It had to be someone who knew I was all the way in Seattle and didn't fear getting caught.

They got away with a bunch of shoes and clothes plus my X-Box but, to my surprise, they didn't take the shoe with the $10,000 in it. I was relieved to still have my money but I felt very uncomfortable and decided to go stay at a hotel. The next morning I informed the apartment manager that my place had been broken into and they didn't seem to care too much. A window was broken and they told me that unless I filed a police report I would have to pay for it. I filed the police report but the police seemed to care about what happened even less than the management of my apartments. The police treated me as if I had broken into someone's place rather than had my place broke into. I wasn't surprised because throughout my whole life every interaction with the police had been negative. They had never helped anyone in my family, only hurt them or arrested them. I didn't expect them to ever find the person who broke into my apartment and honestly if I did expect them to find the person I wouldn't have even filed the police report. I was just doing what I had to do so that my window could be replaced without me being charged for it. There was no investigation or any further contact after filing the police report.

After having my house broken into I realized that it was way too dangerous to be riding around in a Lexus on dubs with a pocket full of money and not have a gun. I reached out to a couple people and bought three guns. I kept one in my apartment, one in my glove box, and one on me. As far as I knew, the person who broke into my apartment had a personal grudge with me. Would they be coming to physically harm me next? I didn't know and I didn't want to risk being caught slipping. There would have been absolutely nothing wrong with me owning these guns besides the fact that I was not yet old enough to apply for a license. I needed them for my protection. For so many people in this country that is perfectly acceptable but for a young black man like me it was something to hide. Shooting myself taught me a great lesson that guns were not toys and with owning them came responsibility.

That summer Mo didn't get picked in the NBA draft. He ended up taking his name out of consideration because he had no guarantee of being selected. As a result, he decided to attend college for one year before entering the draft again. He just didn't know which college to attend. In late July, we decided we were going to go to Kube 93 Summer Jam and when we got back I could help him make his decision on which college to go to.

Summer Jam 2004 was an amazing event but we almost didn't get a chance to experience it. We had booked a hotel room and decided to drive out the night before the concert. It was me, Mo, my cousin Mega, and one of Mega's friends. We left in the middle of the night and Mo volunteered to drive. I was happy with that because we were always riding together and I trusted Mo's driving more than anyone in the world. On the way to Summer Jam he was doing 80-85 miles per hour in the far-left lane when suddenly we saw headlights coming directly at us. Mo reacted immediately and dodged the vehicle that was headed the wrong way on the freeway, but he also lost control of the car and we spun out and flew off the road. We came to a stop safely but I was pissed. We all hopped out, still trying to gather ourselves and make sense out of what had happened. We saw no sign of the car that we had just almost had a deadly head-on collision with. Moments later a cop car pulled up and we explained what happened.

Any time you have four black men interacting with a single cop, that interaction is going to be pretty intense. For some reason cops fear us even when there is no reason to be feared. He questioned us as if we were suspects. Who knows, maybe he thought we were the vehicle that was going the wrong way on the freeway rather than the people who just almost got killed by it.

Despite that near-tragic event on the way to the concert we had a great time. It was the most fun concert I have ever been to. All of the musical acts were great, the women were looking great, we ran into a lot of people that we knew. I even ran into Theresa for the first time since dropping her and her friend off after they walked out of my apartment in the middle of the night.

After Summer Jam, the summer was basically coming to an end. Mo had still not made up his mind about his next move. His phone would often ring with coaches from various colleges on the other end but sometimes he didn't even pick up. I could tell he didn't really want to go to college, he was ready to be a pro. Besides, school is not for everyone. Sometimes when coaches called he would even hand me the phone and I would pretend like I was him. There was a time that I spoke to an assistant coach from the University of Kansas, a national basketball powerhouse. I was pretending to be Mo and the coach was trying to convince me that Kansas was the place to be. Had Mo gone there he would have probably won a national championship and made it to the NBA but it would have most likely required more than one year of college. His mind was set on going for one year and then re-entering the draft.

Eventually, he began getting calls from the head coach at a junior college in Hutchinson Kansas. He was a high-profile recruit so this was not a likely landing place for him. However, he decided that a junior college might be a good setting for him to truly dominate. Worst-case scenario, he could play one year and then transfer to a major university if getting drafted wasn't a possibility. He informed the coach at Hutchinson junior college that he would go there to play basketball as long as they allowed me to come with him.

At the time, I had never thought of college as a possibility for me. My academic background was horrible. I had passed the GED test but I didn't think that my GED would actually lead me to college. I knew that hitting bank licks was not going to last forever. I recently had my apartment broken into and had a near-death experience on the way to Summer Jam so I figured this could be a change for the better. The coach told Mo that if he came to Hutchinson they would make sure that my tuition, meals and dorm were covered just as they would for Mo. This was an opportunity that I could not pass up.

We didn't have long before we had to leave for Kansas as it was already August by the time we decided to go there. School was starting soon and we wanted to be there early to get settled in. I was still under a lease at my apartment and had all my furniture and belongings to deal with. My mom wanted to move from her place so I paid the rent through the end of my lease, which was two months, and let her move in. She agreed to do the final cleaning and have someone move my furniture and other belongings into storage once the lease was up. She was very happy that I was going to be attending college.

Before I left, I sold my guns and got rid of as much stuff as possible. I hit what I believed to be my final bank lick so that I could have some money in my pocket for the trip. Finally, me and Mo packed our bags, filled the trunk of my LS 400, and hopped on the freeway headed toward Hutchinson, Kansas.

8
THERE'S NO PLACE LIKE HOME

When we arrived at Hutchinson the whole coaching staff for the basketball team was outside waiting for us. After we were introduced, they passed us off to one of the returning basketball players for a tour of the campus. I was very happy to be there. Hutchinson was not at all what I expected from a junior college. The fact that they had dorms made it different than many of the community colleges back home. The sports leagues were also extremely competitive and they even played across state lines I believe.

Neither one of us were enrolled at the school yet when we arrived and we also had not yet applied for financial aid, so we both had paperwork to do and a bit of a process to go through when we got there. When we spoke to the coaches on the phone before coming we got the impression that I would be given a scholarship and be taken care of just as Mo was but once we arrived there was no mention of a scholarship for me. However, we got enrolled and set up on a meal plan so we could eat at the cafeteria and we picked our classes so I didn't worry too much. I didn't know anything about this stuff. I just knew we were going to be taken care of.

The dorms were not very nice but I was still excited to move in. Me and Mo were given a small room at the end of the hall with two beds, two desks, and nothing else in it. I was the only non-athlete who was staying in the basketball player's dorms so that was pretty cool of them to keep us together. Pretty much everyone on the basketball team was cool. There were some hilarious personalities around on an everyday basis so that kept things fun. We spent a lot of time in the dorms for the women's softball and volleyball teams as well. There was a great mix of people from all over the US.

We got a lot of attention in Hutchinson. A lot of people around us were impressed by the fact that Mo had been in the NBA draft and was supposed to be re-entering. A lot of other people were impressed by the fact that we were rolling in a Lexus on dubs. We made a lot of friends in a real short period of time.

Hutchinson was a very small town and there was not much to do at all. There was a state fair there shortly after we arrived but besides that the only things to do were mess around on campus or on the weekends there would sometimes be a house party. There was also a nightclub but it was the absolute weirdest mix of people and music imaginable. I have never in life expected to hear hip-hop music and square dancing music in the same nightclub on the same night. There were a lot of cowboy-looking people as well as young hip-hop heads. I guess we were all in the same place because there was nowhere else to go. I can still picture it now how everyone from the basketball team would get in these circles and dance using pretty much just their hands and arms. It was an ok time but nothing like the nightclubs back home.

Once classes started I was excited to begin. I was enrolled in a math class that me and Mo both were in, an acting class, and a weightlifting class. Besides the required math class I pretty much just picked the classes from the catalog that sounded interesting to me. Acting sounded fun and weightlifting was something that I felt I needed at the time because I wanted to try to get in shape. I really enjoyed the acting and weight lifting class but in math I was in over my head. This was not even a college level math class but I still had no idea what I was doing.

Although Kansas was ok, I started to miss being in Washington. I had run out of money and was out there with nothing. Mo, like the rest of the basketball team, was given a job working at the football games but I wasn't included in that. He didn't make much money working anyway. Before coming to Kansas for college I had been making more than enough money to have whatever I wanted. We didn't even have a TV or anything in our dorm. We were really struggling. Sometimes the cafeteria food wasn't even enough to keep us full through the night so we would always end up in the female dorms trying to get one of the girls to buy us some McDonald's. This grew old for me pretty quickly. I didn't like living like this.

I had been spending a lot of time on the phone talking to Theresa. Running into her at Summer Jam shortly before leaving for Kansas had put her back on my radar and I mostly talked to her on the phone because I was bored. There were also two other females I would talk to on the phone a lot while I was in Kansas. One of them was in Oregon and one in California. I never expected anything to come from talking to any of the three considering the distance between us. I wasn't planning on leaving Kansas any time soon.

When it came to Theresa, she clearly had other guys she was actually seeing in person and there were times when it came up through the same friend she was with when I met her. Her friend sure seemed to back-stab her and down-talk her often. However, although me and Theresa talked a lot, to me it was just harmless conversation. Although I wasn't taking it too seriously, especially with me being all the way in Kansas, I eventually started to lead her on and make her think I wanted to be with her. I didn't know when I would even see her again in person and up to that point I had only seen her twice. The first time was the day I met her and the second time was at Summer Jam, so really there was no reason for her to take me seriously.

Come to find out, it wouldn't be as long as I thought before I would be in Tacoma again. By the beginning of October I was flat out homesick. I made a couple phone calls and before you knew it Mo was dropping me off at the airport in Wichita so that I could spend the weekend at home.

The first thing I did when I got off the plane was go visit family. I went to see my mom and my sisters then I went to see my cousins. I made some calls and got my hands on an ATM card so I could get some money. Let's be real, not having money was my biggest issue with being all the way in Kansas. I knew I didn't have time to go through the whole process of hitting a bank lick so I sold the card to someone else who also hit bank licks.

While I was in Tacoma I met up with Theresa and one of her friends at a movie theater. I have never been that "let's go to the movies" type of guy, but I went anyway. I got to the theater late and they were already in there watching Napoleon Dynamite. The movie was so extremely stupid to me but they were enjoying it. I was ready to get on the move so eventually I convinced them to leave. We ended up hanging out for a little while and going our separate ways. Theresa and her friend seemed really immature and goofy but it made for a good time. There was a lot of laughs.

After the weekend was over I went to the Sea-Tac Airport and hopped on a plane back to Wichita. Mo met me at the airport in Wichita with a couple of our friends from the basketball team and we drove back to Hutch. When we got back to Hutchinson I went and bought a TV for me and Mo's room. I also bought a video game console from one of the members of the basketball team named Peanut.

For the first couple days once I got back things were a little bit better. I felt like now that I had gotten my hands on some money I had solved the problems that really led to me feeling homesick. We didn't have to be hungry any more, we finally had some entertainment. However, as the week went on, I decided I was going to fly back home for the weekend again.

When I flew back this time my mom had helped me get a rental car so it was easier for me to get around. After I left my mom, the first person I met with was Theresa. I think at this point I actually started to like her. This was different for me because throughout my life I never allowed myself to have feelings for a female. They would always come and go. None really stuck around long enough for feelings to even occur. There were quite a few signs that Theresa probably wasn't someone I would want to truly make my girlfriend, mostly because of things her so-called friend had told me, but I wanted to be around her. We hung out the whole weekend.

When I got back to Kansas I was informed that my tuition had still not been paid by financial aid. Applying for, and receiving aid was a process that took some time but at this school you cannot continue past a certain date if your tuition is not paid. We talked to the coaches who promised to take care of me just as they would take care of Mo but they offered no solutions or even assistance. I began to realize that they told us what we wanted to hear in order to get Mo to come to their school. They had no intention of giving me any type of scholarship or helping me pay for my tuition, my meals, or my dorm. Tuition alone was in the thousands of dollars. When you add the dorm and meal plan to it the price was through the roof. Less than three months after arriving in Kansas, I was going to have to leave.

I thought that having a friend who was a highly-recruited basketball player had finally provided me with an opportunity to move past my disadvantaged background and make something of myself. In my mind, I was there to earn a college degree. Obviously, had things gone as planned, Mo would have been entering the NBA draft the next year and we would have both left, but I wasn't thinking that far ahead.

All I knew at this point was that I was basically back at square one. I gave up everything for this opportunity. I no longer had a place to live of my own. I didn't have any money. I didn't have a lot of options. I had to go back home, but the thing is there was no place to call home.

On October 30th, 2004, I packed my stuff again to travel across the country. The major difference is that before, I was leaving with my best friend to pursue what could have been a life-changing opportunity. Now, I was headed back to Washington with no idea what I would do with myself. My older sister Nikki told me I could stay with her as long as I needed so at least I would have a roof over my head. Although I was grateful, this wasn't what I wanted after having my own place.

When I came to Kansas I didn't mind the 1,800 miles and 30-hours long drive because I had help and good company along the way. Going back, I was near broke and all alone because Mo didn't run into the same problems I did. His scholarship took care of everything for him. If I could afford it I would have let Mo have my Lexus and flew back but I didn't even have much more than gas money or know where my next dollar would come from.

Not even an hour into my return trip it had already went bad. I wanted to get back to Washington as fast as possible so I was driving near 100 miles per hour when I was pulled over for speeding. I never had insurance so I could have been given a huge ticket but luckily, I was issued a warning for that and only ticketed for speeding. After getting pulled over I made it through Colorado and into Wyoming without issue before things turned bad again.

At one point while I was driving through Wyoming it was very dark and thick snowflakes made it hard to see what was in front of me. There were not a whole lot of cars out but the ones that were out were driving extremely slow. I noticed a few cars were stuck on the side of the freeway, some not even facing the right direction. I was driving in the far-left lane and there was a car in front of me going so slow that I felt like I would have never made it home. I didn't believe it was necessary to go as slow as this car was going so I decided I was going to pass. With us being in the far-left lane I had no choice but to go around this car to the right. When I went to pass the car, I had to press the accelerator a little harder than I had been and when I did I completely lost control of my car. I was trying to control the steering while also having my foot on the brakes but it was a lost cause. I spun in 2-3 full circles before coming to a stop in what seemed like maybe 2-3 feet of snow on the side of the freeway.

This reminded me a lot of what had happened on the way to Summer Jam just months earlier. Somehow, I had avoided injury and avoided any damage to the car but I was still shook up. The major difference this time was that I was stuck. My cellphone had no reception so I couldn't call for help but I had just passed another car that was stuck and being helped by a tow truck. I decided that I would walk back to where that car was and see if I could get the tow truck driver to help me next.

It wasn't a far walk to get to the spot where the tow truck was, but in deep snow and freezing cold it seemed like a far walk. The car being pulled out by the tow truck was pretty much in the same position my car was in so that gave me hope that I could get back on the road pretty quickly. When I approached the tow truck driver he told me he would help me next but the cost would be $150. I told him that I didn't have a lot of money and he agreed to do it for half the price. Before long he had pulled my car out of the deep snow and back onto the freeway. I drove extremely slow until I reached a rest area where I decided to sleep until daylight. When I woke up, I still had a little over half of my trip left but it went smoothly and without incident the rest of the way.

Once I was back in Tacoma I had settled in at my sister's house. I didn't really want to hit bank licks because I just wanted to live a normal life and be successful. I thought college was my way out of poverty but now I was forced to come up with a different plan. However, instead of planning and executing, I was just stagnant.

Now that we weren't so far away from each other I began hanging with Theresa and she had officially became my first girlfriend. I had told her she was my girl while I was still in Kansas but neither one of us respected that or took it seriously. Now, we were actually able to see each other regularly so it was more real.

After being back less than a month, Theresa hit me with some life-changing news. I was completely caught off guard when she told me that she was pregnant with my child. I was really nervous about having a kid on the way being in the position I was in. I also didn't know what to think because I knew she was still talking to and seeing other guys while I was in Kansas and I didn't know if I could trust that the kid was mine. She assured me that she hadn't had sex with anyone else since the beginning of the Summer so I took her word for it.

With the realization that I had a kid on the way I felt like I had no option but to go as hard as possible with the bank lick. I was going to need to get a place as soon as possible and I wanted to be able to provide my child with everything he would need. I didn't know of any other way to get money besides hustling. Getting a job wasn't even on my radar.

The same weekend that I found out Theresa was pregnant I happened to be hanging out with the same homegirl I was with when I shot myself back when I was living on Hilltop. Ironically, I also had on a pair of those Makaveli jeans with Tupac's face on them just like I had on the day I shot myself. Even more ironic, her birthday was on the day Tupac died, September 13th. Theresa for some reason tried convincing me to stay home that night but I wanted to go out so I did. We didn't live together and her influence was limited over the phone.

I drove to Seattle with my homegirl and a mutual friend of ours. We drove from spot to spot but none of them really seemed to be popping. I was still only 19 years old so I wasn't old enough to go inside of 21 and up establishments, which meant our options were limited. Although I wasn't old enough to go in, I still liked to drive by some of the bars and nightclubs for 21 and up crowds, just to be seen. If it looked packed and there were a lot of people around I loved to parking lot pimp. For those who don't know what that means, I would post up outside by my car and talk to females.

It was getting close to closing time for the Seattle bars and clubs which is at 2 AM. We decided to drive through Belltown and into Pioneer Square past all the bars there. When we rolled past one of the popular bars in Belltown we had the windows down and the music blasting and this guy yelled out the my homegirl "bitch that's not your hair". When she heard that she got all hyped and started hanging out the window talking shit back. I thought it was pretty funny but didn't think much else of it. I saw my cousin Kadafi so I decided to park so I could go say what's up to him.

By the time I parked and got to where I saw my cousin he was gone. I didn't see him anywhere. I stood there watching as a fight broke out until I saw one of the dudes who was fighting start shooting in the air. The loud gunshots caused the crowd to scatter. I hit the corner and made sure I found the people I came with and we went back to the car and left.

I hopped on I-5 headed back toward Tacoma. We had the music blasting and there was a video playing on the TV screen I had installed in my review mirror. Although we didn't go inside of any of the clubs it was still cool just to hang out and drive around so I considered this to be a solid night. By the time we were on the freeway heading south it was around 3 AM and we were all tired. Both of my passengers had fallen asleep. I was doing around 60 in the second to left lane, next to the carpool lane which was far left. Suddenly a red van pulled behind me and then went switched into the carpool lane, as if to pass me.

When the van got on the side of me I saw an arm reach out of the passenger window, point a gun my direction, and let loose. Pop! Pop! Pop! Pop! Pop! Pop! Pop! I felt the burn. I was hit. Although I felt the pain of the bullet, I had no idea the extent of the damage. I yelled out, "this muthafucka just shot me." My passengers were awakened by the gunfire but luckily neither one of them had been hit. After emptying a whole clip into my Lexus, the van sped off as I slowed down and took the next exit.

Had it not been for the low-profile tires, my car would have been out of commission right there on the freeway. Luckily, I was able to get off and park in a parking lot. When I got out the car the situation seemed so familiar. My leg was covered in blood and there was a hole in Tupac's face on my jeans. This time I had gotten lucky, the bullet that hit me did not go through, it had only grazed me knee.

The crazy thing is, it grazed my knee at the exact spot where the bullet left when I shot myself. How insane is that to take a bullet once again while in the car with the same person, wearing the same type of jeans? These jeans also just so happened to have Tupac's face on them. Tupac just so happened to get shot while riding in a car. My homegirl's birthday just so happens to be the day that Tupac died. Weird, right?

Once I got off the freeway I immediately called my cousins, who called some friends, and within a matter of time that parking lot was full of people who had my back. There were bullet holes in my rims, in my door, in the back of my car, in the front of my car, in the headlights, pretty much all over. I was lucky to be alive. The people I had with me were lucky to be alive. Really, some might say I wasn't lucky at all. Some might say that I am blessed and had God or Angels watching over me. I have no idea who it was who tried to take my life that day or why. All I know is that they failed. Dying that day was not God's plan for me.

9
A WHOLE 'NOTHER LEVEL

When I found out that Theresa was pregnant with my first kid that motivated me to make as much money as possible. Once someone tried to take my life, that motivated me even more. I decided that I wasn't going to be shook up and stop hustling just because the way I was shining might have made me a target. I decided that I was going to shine even brighter and if that made people want to kill me then so be it. I wasn't going to live my life scared.

I really loved that Lexus LS 400 but since it was full of bullet holes it had to go. I traded it in for an Eddie Bauer edition 2000 Ford Expedition. I had always wanted a big truck and this one was nice. I still hated Fords because every Ford I ever had up to this point ended up with either a blown head gasket or a blown transmission. However, I had to get rid of that Lexus and this was what caught my eye at the time.

By December of 2004 I had found an apartment in Puyallup and I had Theresa and her daughter move in with me. I immediately began to treat her daughter as my own. With Nariya living under the same roof as me, I was in a position where I played a major role in caring for her and I essentially became a dad overnight.

I didn't know anything about being a parent. I didn't really have a lot of great role models around when it came to parenting. I had to pretty much learn as I went along. Nariya was only one year old when she moved in with me and still wearing diapers and learning how to talk so although she wasn't biologically mine, I considered her to be my first kid. All of my friends and family treated her as if she was my kid as well.

Once Theresa moved in with me she started to get a closer view of my hustle. Slowly but surely, she began to get involved in the bank licks that I was hitting. At first, she started by just writing checks out for me, eventually she started making the deposits, and then she ended up getting ATM cards. She also helped me pull the money out of the bank accounts once the checks cleared.

Once we became a tandem the money started pouring in like never before. I thought I was making a lot of money before ,but once I moved to Puyallup the money started coming in on a whole new level. Previously, I was a one-man show. I had to do everything myself from getting the cards, to writing checks and making deposits. Once I had her help doing this the whole operation became a lot more efficient. It still wasn't highly organized or even calculated but together we got a lot more done in terms of criminal activity.

There was never any pressure for Theresa to get involved with bank licks. She made the decision on her own and was motivated by the same thing that motivated me to do it, money. She liked being able to go to the mall or any store and be able to buy anything she wanted with no limits. She liked the fact that we had a nice apartment with a big screen TV and nice furniture. She loved the fact that her daughter had everything she could possibly desire and our son that she was pregnant with was going to have the same.

While Theresa was pregnant I spent most of my time chasing money. Because of my lifestyle, I spent a lot of time around other females. Most of the people I got bank cards from were money-hungry females who were impressed by my possessions. This was the lifestyle she was going to have to deal with if she was going to be in a relationship with someone like me and she still chose to stick around.

Every now and then I would get into an argument with Theresa about some girl and sometimes it would lead to her packing her stuff and going back to her mom's house. She would always come back before long. It seemed like most of the time she would come back with a bank card in hand and I was blinded by the money so any issues I may have had would go away when I saw that. There was no way she was going to stop me from being around other females because money had to be made so these fights were rare.

During the short time that I lived in Puyallup, I made and wasted more money than most people I know would make in five years. When

I lived in Steilacoom it would take me a while to stack up $10,000-$15,000. However, living in Puyallup, there were days when I made more than that. I traded in the Piercing Pagoda jewelry for much more expensive pieces. I always liked to wear a gold chain and I didn't realize how low quality the stuff I was wearing previously was until I started getting my hands on large amounts of money.

I would often buy Theresa diamonds as a gift but it seems like no matter what I bought her it would eventually come up missing. I remember there was a time that I bought her a very nice and expensive diamond bracelet that she left lying around the house and someone stole it. The sad part is it was most likely stolen by someone that we knew pretty well and had at our house multiple times. Expensive items that weren't stolen would sometimes still come up missing after being misplaced.

Once I started touching large amounts of cash that Ford Expedition obviously wasn't enough anymore. I got rid of the Expedition and got a 1997 E 420 Mercedes Benz. I always referred to it as the "bubble-eye Benz". While I had this car I also bought a 1995 GS 300 Lexus. I put the Benz on 20-inch rims and put a TV screen with a navigation system in the dash. The Lexus came with an after-market pop-out TV screen already in the dash so all I had to do to that car was put it on dub spinners.

Eventually I missed having a truck. My cousin had a 1995 Chevrolet Suburban for sale so I bought that from him just to help him out. I didn't really like the Suburban so I traded that with cash for a much nicer 1995 Chevrolet Tahoe. The Tahoe had nice leather interior and was all black. I threw some black with chrome 22 inch rims on there and also added an after-market alarm with a pager that shows which part of your car was broken into while also functioning as a remote starter. I had beats in the trunk of the Tahoe as well.

Theresa had never drove when we moved in together but I wanted her to learn so I had bought her an old and small Saturn that she could learn in. Once she learned how to drive I bought her a 2001 Ford Taurus. Although she learned how to drive, she never got her license. Plus, she didn't drive very well and I was always scared when I rode with her so I didn't want to spend too much money on her car. However, she could always drive the other cars we had if she wanted to. I always had the luxury cars in my name and I was the main one to drive them but they were really both of ours, especially considering how valuable she had become in regards to hitting bank licks.

Around May 2005, the amount of money I was making had went through the roof. I always had at least $20,000-$30,000 put up somewhere. I decided that it was time for me to elevate my car game to a whole new level. I had recently bought a Cadillac STS but I started to realize that with the type of money I had I could start looking at buying my dream car. My dream car at the time was a BMW 745 but I always thought it was untouchable. I felt that it would always be a dream. This was the car that millionaires were driving at the time. Every rapper, every athlete, and every celebrity had one.

I accepted the fact that I would not be hopping in my dream car any time soon and I settled for a 2000 Mercedes Benz S 430. In order to get this car I had to trade in my bubble-eye Benz and my GS Lexus along with $25,000 cash. When I got behind the wheel of my S-Class Benz I was down to about $10,000 but I felt rich. I felt like I had finally made it. I felt like I was going to be on for life and would never fall off. I immediately dipped into the money I had left and threw some dub spinners on the Benz and put beats in the trunk. When I had this car, it was the best and most expensive car that anyone I knew ever had and I was only 20-years old.

After I had the S 430 for a short time I was not satisfied. My rims scraped a lot when I hit even a small bump in the road and the spinners were the cheap adapters that hardly even spin. I remember going to Portland and being embarrassed that I was riding in this car. I knew I would take a big loss if I got rid of it but that's just something I was going to have to do. In June 2005 I happened to be looking on Auto Trader and I found a car I really wanted for what seemed like an acceptable price.

What I found was a beautiful, blue, 2002 BMW 745i in Fremont, California. My dream car! I called the dealership and they said they would be willing to accept my S Class as a trade-in along with $10,000 cash. I couldn't believe that the price on the 745 was so much lower than all the other 745s out there. I told Theresa to find a baby sitter for Nariya and we hopped on I-5 south headed toward Fremont to trade in my S 430 Benz for a BMW 745.

The drive from Puyallup to the Bay Area was nothing compared to the drive I had made alone from Kansas. I was excited to be going to get this car but I was also skeptical because as I had mentioned, this was a rich man's car. When we got to Fremont it was night time so we got a hotel room and some food and chilled for the night. Right when the dealership opened in the morning we went straight there.

When I got to the dealership I immediately noticed the car I drove all this way for. It was beautiful and the price tag was true to what I saw online. The guy working at the dealership tossed me the keys and I hopped in for a test drive. I was so excited to even be sitting in this car. Once I had to push a button to start the car, and noticed that it had voice control, I just had to have it. I always liked technology and gadgets and this car had so many features that it blew me away.

Once I returned from the test drive I was ready to do the deal but the dealer informed me that he would need to inspect the car I was trading in. Once they came back from inspection he told me that I would have to get him $20,000 instead of $10,000 if I wanted to do the trade. I honestly didn't understand why the price would have doubled from what I was told over the phone but I was so anxious and had come so far that I immediately agreed. I didn't have the full $20,000 on me so I gave them $15,000 and they allowed me to pay the rest once I got to my stash back home in Washington.

Shortly after getting home, Theresa went to her cousin's house to get her hair braided and while she was getting her hair done she went into labor. Our son, Amare, was born on June 24th, 2005 at St. Joseph's hospital in Tacoma. I was very scared leading up to the birth as her due date was still very far away.

Amare was born premature and was really small with a low birth weight. He had to be fed through a tube in his nose and stayed in the hospital for a week. I was there with Theresa for most of that week but I also did quite a bit of running around, mostly chasing money. I didn't want to pass up any opportunities, especially because my son had just been born. I was very relieved and happy once he gained some weight and we were allowed to bring him home.

When my son was born, I wasn't quite prepared. I was under the impression that I still had quite some time to get ready. We had been buying things and money wasn't an issue so we had everything we needed for him, but I wasn't quite ready yet mentally. Plus, with him being pre-mature and so small, I was scared to death. I honestly didn't want to touch him because he was so fragile and I thought I would hurt him.

Once I had adjusted to having a new little baby enter things started to get back to normal. I was right back to the everyday grind. I had my dream car and all I wanted to do was be seen in it. Part of me just wanted to stunt on the competition. Mostly, I wanted to get out there and use my car to my advantage to make even more money. I put some 22-inch chrome rims on my 7 series and it really just came to life. The car had so many features that I didn't need to do anything else to it. I knew that this car could be used as a magnet to attract females and money.

About one month after I bought my first 745, I started to get that itch again. I felt like I needed a new car once again. The one I had was nice, but it wasn't really the right color for me. I decided that I was going to trade my 745 for another 745 in a different color.

I found this dealership in Bellevue that not only had a 745 in a different color, they actually had one with far more features. I had no idea that the first 745 I had was not fully loaded. There were so many features that I didn't know there was room for any sort of improvement. The new one that I found also had less miles. I paid $15,000 to trade-in the car I had just recently drove all the way to California to purchase, for another car that was the same exact year, make, and model. I ended up keeping the same 22s from the old car but I still spent a bunch of money installing drop-down TV screens from the roof with an X-Box 360 connected to them that was installed in a compartment in the trunk. I also had mirror tints installed.

When it came to buying these cars I only did it because I was really young and dumb. The large amounts of money that I ran through buying the cars, rims, speakers, tvs and other features should have been saved and put away somewhere. I didn't have many positive influences in my life. I didn't have anyone giving me advice. I really just didn't know any better and I looked at flashy things as a way to lend credibility when I would have to convince someone to part with their bank card or checks. People are unlikely to place their faith in someone who is broke but when they saw me pull up in a foreign luxury car on big shiny rims it was a whole different story.

Either way, I took major losses every time I traded a car in. My cars were what I became known for. People started to talk about me having a 745 everywhere I went. That was my claim to fame. There are not a lot of people who are able to own a car like that before they are old enough to drink without being some sort of celebrity but I would have much preferred to have been known for starting a successful business or saving and investing in my future.

The sad truth is that when people are hustling and getting money illegally they probably won't do much of anything with it. You don't see a lot of people owning property and businesses using money that they got illegally. If they do, then anything they thought they accomplished could be snatched away at any moment. If you buy a business or property with money that you obtained illegally then you will never feel comfortable because those things can be seized. I thought I was winning but in reality, I was headed toward disaster and losing.

When the money comes fast it is for sure to go fast. Dirty money will not get you anywhere in life. It's hard to even respect money when you aren't working hard for it. There are people who spend 40 hours per week making less than $15,000-$20,000 per year and although they might live paycheck to paycheck they are still able to get by. It's sad that I have been able to touch that type of money in a day and would end up with nothing to show for it a month later.

In the Summer of 2005 my life was changed with the birth of my son. Although I had already been playing a major role in raising his big sister, he was my first biological kid. After his birth, I was right back to my old ways because in my mind chasing money was something that could never stop.

However, as time went by, I started wanting to be a better man. I wanted to stop always being on the go and chasing money. I wanted to stop being a negative presence around my son. Although I was a good man and a good father, I was still living a criminal lifestyle. I also was allowing the people around me and even music to influence me in a negative way.

I still didn't drink alcohol but I began smoking a lot of weed after staying away from it until the age of 20. I had tried it once with Jay but I ended up doing a bunch of stupid stuff and tried to climb up Key Arena. I didn't really like the feeling at all and it made me paranoid. I used to always think it was stupid to want to feel that way. However, my cousin Kadafi had an ounce that he was trying to get rid of so I took it off his hands to help him out and from that day forward I was not just smoking weed, but I was smoking large amounts of weed.

During this time, I listened to a Bay Area rapper named Mac Dre on an everyday basis and listening to his music was just different than other music for some reason. When I listened to Mac Dre I actually wanted to do what he was talking about. I went from refusing to touch any drugs to popping ecstasy pills. I didn't do it a whole lot but I did it and that was so unlike me. Seattle and Tacoma during this time had a lot of young people who were Mac Dre fans who mimicked everything Mac Dre did. For me it felt amazing to be riding in my 745 listening to Mac Dre say "We in the 7-series beamer, it's me and Nickatina, ready to sexual harass a bitch, like Martin did Gina." I would usually be with one of my boys looking for some females so it's like Mac Dre was rapping my life. I don't think I know a single person my age from Seattle or Tacoma who has never mimicked Mac Dre and popped an E pill, drove their car while hanging out the sun roof, and did the Thizzelle Dance. I'm sure there are a bunch out there who grew up like squares and were able to avoid the influence but most of the people I know, who grew up like me, were all doing the same things that I was.

I knew that the guy who I was right then and there, was not the guy who I wanted my son to look up to. I planned on being in his life and staying in his life so I knew that everything I did would teach him and help mold the person he would become. I had changes to make. I had to do better.

The bank licks started coming slower and slower after the summer of 2005. I began to put in a lot less effort. I was tired. By November of 2005 we had a notice on our door informing us that our lease would not be renewed and we had to be out by the end of the month. I decided that once we moved, our lives were going to be different. My run with bank licks was done.

10
FALLING OFF

Once our lease was up we packed our stuff and moved in with my sister Sareeta in Lakewood. She had a big family herself. She had her daughter, two twin toddlers who were still in diapers, and a brand new baby boy. Although she had a big family, the downstairs portion of her house was not being used so there was room for me, Theresa, Nariya, and Amare. She gave us the whole downstairs and we settled in and got comfortable.

Theresa had gotten a job at Arby's and I was pretty much doing nothing with my life, just watching the kids. By the time January rolled around people had started going to jail for hitting bank licks and it made the news so I was scared to leave the house. Once I saw that people were getting arrested there was no chance of me going back to hitting bank licks. I was going to need to figure out something because my life had no direction.

It was around this time when Theresa and I had gotten into a petty argument and she decided to go hang out with her so-called best friend. They decided to convince some guy to give them his bank card so they could hit a bank lick. Theresa knew I was done with bank licks at the time. I wanted nothing to do with them, however, she made the decision that she wasn't done. They convinced this guy to give up his bank card and they hit a bank lick on his account that hardly made them any money.

Not long after Theresa and her friends hit this bank lick, detectives started popping up at her mom's house looking for her. We were scared to death. Eventually we decided that the best thing for us to do would be to leave the state so we made arrangements for the kids to stay with her mom and we hopped on the freeway to go to California.

While we were in California we completely ignored what was going on back home and tried to have fun. We were basically on a vacation. Plus, it was Theresa's birthday so we wanted to celebrate. We went to Universal

Studios and to a Lakers vs Clippers game. We drove around Beverly Hills and did a lot of sight-seeing. Of course, I had to go eat at Roscoe's Chicken & Waffles as well. We had no idea what the future held for us but it didn't matter at the time.

After about 5 days in California, we decided that we were going to go to Washington to get the kids, and then move permanently to Portland. When we got back to Washington we were very paranoid and we were trying not to be seen. Although it was a Gig Harbor police officer that had been looking for Theresa, we had no idea what the extent of their investigation was. One thing was for sure, we didn't want to find out.

I knew that riding in a 745 was no longer a good idea. I needed a different car. I had come to be known for the cars I was driving and I didn't want to give the police or any detectives who might be looking for me an easy way to find me. I started looking for quick ways to get rid of the car without taking too big of a loss. Eventually, I found a car dealership out north of Seattle that offered me $10,000 cash and a 2002 Lexus LS 430 in exchange so I jumped on it. The Lexus had a $30,000 price tag on it and I was running low on money so the $10,000 is exactly what we needed to relocate my family to Oregon.

We gathered up our stuff again and In March of 2006, right before my 21st birthday, we had moved in with my dad in Beaverton. Because we had two vehicles I had to drive down there, catch the Greyhound back, and then drive there again, but I didn't mind. This was just what we had to do if we were going to have a chance at starting our lives over. As far as we knew, neither one of us had a warrant for our arrest. The detectives from Gig Harbor wanted to talk with Theresa, but as far as I knew, I was not a wanted man. I believed we had a good shot at getting away with all we had done and moving on as if nothing happened.

Once we got settled in with my dad, Theresa found a job working at Quiznos nearby. I spent most of my day sitting around with the kids, playing video games, and making rap songs on my computer. My life pretty much had no direction and I was lost and confused in regards to what I wanted to do with myself. Eventually, I decided that I was going to wait until the Fall and start school at Portland Community College. I filled out the FAFSA and my application for admission was approved so I just had to chill until the time came to start college.

Any time I went searching for a way out of my criminal lifestyle I would always seek an education. It just came natural and I credit my dad for instilling in me a thirst for knowledge. I made the decision to use education as a tool to better my life first when I got my GED, then when I had went to Kansas, and now I was enrolling at PCC. It became obvious to me that unless I had earned an education my options would always be limited. I knew I had a lot of potential but it was all going to waste. Without an education, I could have done like Theresa and pursued a job at a fast-food restaurant but my personal standards just wouldn't allow it. There was no way I was going to go from the type of money I had been making to working for minimum wage. Not only that, I have just never been that type of person to settle for less than I am worth and especially if it would make me feel degraded in the process. I do not knock fast-food workers or hard laborers but those are things I just could not and would not allow myself to do. Sometimes humility is not a good thing and can keep you from recognizing your true potential and I don't feel any need to humble myself and accept a life of poverty and misery.

Due to my high-standards and refusal to settle for less than my perceived self-worth, I ended up basically contributing nothing to my family financially. Obviously, there was value in me being with the kids while Theresa was at work but I had essentially sat stagnant while waiting for school to start. I ended up selling my Tahoe for $5,000 because we didn't really have anywhere to keep it. It was awkward enough pulling up to my dad's poor and broke down apartment complex in a Lexus but it was even worse having that truck there because the rims and beats attracted a lot of attention. The LS 430 was a nice and expensive car but it was on stock wheels with no tinted windows and didn't attract a lot of attention at all.

We lived with my dad for several months before finally deciding to find a place of our own. We hadn't been arrested yet and if the police were looking for us, we sure didn't know about it. The detective had stopped showing up looking for Theresa so we thought they had given up. My sister Nikki came down and helped me look for a place that we were going to put in her name just in case they were still looking for us. We didn't have any luck so she went back to Washington. Eventually we got comfortable enough and felt safe enough to take that bold step and get a place in our own names.

Not much time had passed before we found a cheap apartment on Lombard avenue in Portland that was willing to let us move in right away. We were happy to accept anything at the time so we jumped at the opportunity. I was already accepted at PCC and Theresa had been getting more hours at work so we felt that life could only get better for us. Every now and then I got that itch to get back to hitting bank licks but I was able to resist the temptation. I figured that if we just continued to take care of our kids and stay away from negativity then opportunity would have to come eventually. Getting our own place was progress and I just knew that things would only get better from there.

Unfortunately, I was completely wrong. Things were only about to get worse for our family. Not even two weeks after we moved into our new apartment I got a call from an inmate at the Washington County jail. That inmate was Theresa.

Apparently, when she tried to leave work that night, the car wouldn't start. A stranger helped and gave her a jump so she was able to get the car running, however, she had turned off the automatic headlights. When you are used to driving a vehicle that automatically turns the lights on and off for you, and somehow that feature gets turned off, it is very easy to drive off and not notice. Immediately when Theresa pulled out of the parking lot without the lights on, she was pulled over by a cop. Theresa had no license and no insurance so she was given $1,000 in traffic tickets for that. She also had four felony warrants out of Pierce County for money laundering.

When I spoked to Theresa on the phone I told her not to talk to any police officers and that I would come bail her out immediately. Little did I know, I was not going to be able to bail her out until she was extradited and sent back to Tacoma. It took about a week for them extradite her and she had to stop at several different jails on the way. Once she went to court in Tacoma, her bail was set at $30,000 and I gave her mom the $3,000 required to bail her out.

Once Theresa was released on bail, I immediately went to pick her up. I was paranoid but I was also curious to know exactly what happened and what was going to happen. She told me that the detectives knew all about me and they knew everything we had done. I was very confused as to how that is possible. She informed me that she told them the truth once they confronted her with evidence of checks that had been written and money orders that were deposited into her bank account. I was pissed off because I told her not to talk to them at all. If the police already know everything then why would they even need to talk to her? People have rights that protect them from self-incrimination but she was intimidated and threatened with not seeing her children again and in that situation it's easy to feel like your rights don't exist. Her four money laundering charges magically went away and were replaced with 30 new charges including theft, forgery, and identity theft. I always thought that when someone snitches they get their charges dismissed but snitching only got her in deeper trouble because she snitched on herself just as much as she had snitched on me.

A lot of men in my position would have wanted nothing to do with a woman or anyone else for that matter who had just snitched on them. However, I have always been a reasonable guy. I knew that she would have never done any of this stuff had it not been for me. I was the one who introduced her to bank licks. I was the one who made this a part of her life.

She would have never been going into the bank cashing money orders, on camera, using her name and bank account, if I didn't ask her to do it. She was a square. Although I expected more loyalty and she should have made a smarter decision in regards to exercising her rights rather than incriminating herself, she wasn't subject to any type of street code.

I would have to be a damn fool to think that a female who has never been from or part of a street culture would follow the street code. Almost every guy I know of who got a square female involved in anything that got her sent to jail ended up getting snitched on by her. It's a part of the game. If you don't want to get told on by a square you need to make sure that no square is in a position to tell on you.

Theresa told me that the police knew about all the money I was making, they knew about the cars I was driving, and they even knew about our apartment in Portland. I was led to believe that she wasn't in a room offering up all sorts of information but at times she was presented with evidence that she couldn't deny so she didn't. I didn't have anything but her word to go from so I was stuck being unsure of the extent of her betrayal for the time being.

I felt crossed by Theresa but at the same time I decided I wasn't going to cut her off and run. I decided that the best thing for me to do was to make sure she knew I wasn't going to abandon her. The way my life was at the time it had been many months since I last participated in any bank lick. I had no criminal history. I figured that if I turned myself in, that would be the best way to handle the situation but first I would have to hire a lawyer. I definitely wasn't going to be next in line to be driving down the street and get hauled from jail to jail until I made it back to Tacoma to face charges.

Since the detectives back in Tacoma knew about our apartment in Portland, living there was no longer an option. We immediately went to get everything that was most important to us and left everything else to be cleared out by my mom and sisters. My family was very supportive of me so although they lived in Tacoma they didn't mind coming to Portland to help me.

My mom and my sister Nikki essentially became my chauffeurs. I was too scared to drive at all and refused to get behind the wheel of a car. I had taken my Lexus LS 430 and sold it to a car dealership for $20,000 cash and a minivan. By that time, that was all I had left. I had my mom and my sister hold on to the money and they would drop me and Theresa off at random hotels for the night. A large amount of the $20,000 that I got for my Lexus went to hotels.

Every now and then Theresa would have a court date to go to and every single time I would be paranoid. I was worried that they were going to keep her for whatever reason. My other concern was that they might follow her to try to get to me. Whenever she would go to court I would be so happy to see her again afterwards. Most of the court dates seemed like a complete waste of time. All they would do is set another court date.

Eventually, it was my turn to face the music. I was referred to a well-known lawyer in the Tacoma area by a friend of mine who had previously retained his services. I was told that this guy was the best around and that he would be sure to get me a good result. I had never dealt with the criminal justice system before so I just took his word for it. I set up a meeting and paid a $7,500 retainer, my warrant was quashed, and an arraignment hearing was set up for October 3rd, 2006.

Once my court date was set up I was very nervous. I really didn't know what to expect once I walked in there. Everyone I knew tried to convince me that because I had never been in trouble before I wasn't going to be looking at much time. A lot of people also tried to convince me that the judge was going to let me go on personal recognizance or with a bail similar to Theresa's $30,000. It didn't matter what anybody had to say because I was still worried and control of my life was out of my hands.

On October 2nd, 2006, my sister Nikki gave birth to a miracle baby. Despite several failed pregnancies and believing that she would never have a child she had finally been able to experience the joy of being a mother. She had diabetes since childhood and she didn't quite eat right or do what she needed to do in order to be healthy enough to have a successful pregnancy in the past so she felt extremely blessed. Her child was born with low birth weight, heart problems and deformities in his head and ears but he was here. I wanted to go see him so bad the day he was born but I decided that I would wait until after my court date the next day.

When I went to court the next day I had my mom, my step-dad, Theresa, my kids, and my sisters with me. They were there to show their support but also to show the judge that I had loved ones who cared about me. I honestly had second thoughts about going through with it. I didn't really know anyone who ever voluntarily walked into a courtroom to face felony charges. Most people I know run from the law for as long as they possibly can. I guess I was just naïve and believed that I would be rewarded for doing the right thing, besides I always thought I would be presumed innocent until proven guilty, whatever that means.

I sat and watched the judge arraign accused person after accused person. Several people were already in custody, some were released with the charges dropped. Other people who had walked in the courtroom as I had that day were sent to jail. Some people were given low bails, some people were given high bails, some people were given no bail. There was a variety of different charges and the people accused had a variety of different backgrounds but the judge seemed to randomly decide how to handle each individual case.

I still had a chance to head for the door. Each time I saw someone get cuffed up I pictured it being me. I had never been to jail before at this point. I was scared to find out what it was like being in a county jail. I wasn't scared of physical harm, I was scared of being locked in a cage away from my loved ones for an unspecified amount of time.

After sitting anxiously in the courtroom for what seemed like ages, it was finally my turn. They called out my name and I nervously walked up to face the judge. About a year and a half before this I had taken Mak to court in Puyallup and when he was cuffed by the bailiff after the judge ordered him to be detained, he ran out of the courtroom and got away. I was trying to think about how I might do the same. My mind was not clear at all. Thoughts were racing. Then, I got to listen to the prosecutor paint the worst possible picture of me.

I was accused of being a flight risk and a threat to others. I was made to look like the worst person in the world. This prosecutor had never met me, never had any type of interactions with me, and never spoke to my family but she appeared to think they knew all about me. The prosecutor had me all wrong. It seems like it should have been clear to the judge that I am not a flight risk and that everything the prosecutor had to say was unproven accusations but that wasn't the case.

The judge obviously soaked up everything the prosecutor said as a fact because despite me having no criminal history, having never been to jail before, and having turned myself in, I was ordered to be detained pending trial with a $100,000 bail. I also was given a no-contact order with Theresa, who had my children.

I feel like one of the main functions of the criminal justice system is to break up families. I don't know how they could justify giving a father a no-contact order with the mother of his children. I understand that they want a conviction but they are destroying lives. The majority of young couples that they do this to are not even going to respect the court's decision when it comes to these things. In my opinion, no one should be forced to cut off communication with someone they are in a long-term relationship with that has their children. Legality and morality are two completely different things and although the court gets to decides what is legal, them issuing this no-contact order was far more immoral than if I chose not to follow it. In addition to being given a no-contact with Theresa, I was also given a no-contact order with two people I knew, but didn't do business with, who had absolutely nothing to do with my case.

When I looked back at my family, a tear fell out of my eye. I was going to jail. With my bail set so high I figured I was never getting out. My lawyer was given almost all the money I had left so I definitely didn't have the $10,000 to get out. Even if I did have the $10,000, I wouldn't have had anyone who can co-sign with collateral equaling the $100,000. I was stuck. Innocent until proven guilty didn't mean anything for me.

Once they cuffed me I was taken to a back room in the courthouse and ultimately went through the booking process. I had to take a mugshot, get my fingerprints taken, and change into the degrading pink clothing that they make inmates wear at the Pierce County Jail. I was given the opportunity to make phone calls and provided with a sandwich and an apple while I waited to be taken to a receiving unit. I felt like my life had just ended.

11
THE COUNTY

The walk from booking to the units where inmates are housed was extremely depressing. They took several of us at a time to walk down the long cold hallways that seemed like they would never end. I almost feel like they designed this walk to be demoralizing. The longer we walked, chained together like animals, the further we were away from freedom. I had no idea what would be at the end of this journey. I almost felt like a slave, a member of a chain gang.

The receiving unit didn't have a lot of people in it when I got there. The first thing I did was make my bed with the sheet and blanket they gave me. I was also provided with a bin and a cup for water while I was in booking. After I made my bed I just sat there looking around. This wasn't quite what I expected jail to look like. I expected to be put in a cell but instead there was a big open room with a lot of bunks. I was in what they called the "new jail" which was for people who were classified as being less of a threat than those in the "old jail".

After a couple hours in receiving I was told to "roll up", which meant pack my stuff. It was time for me to go to the unit that would become my new home while I went through the court process. I packed my things and was taken upstairs to a unit that had a lot more people and a lot more activity.

When I got to my unit I saw people watching TV, working out, playing cards, and playing chess. I actually saw people smiling and laughing. I wondered to myself how people could be so happy in jail. Maybe it wasn't going to be that bad after all.

I was told which bunk was mine and as I was making my way to it I saw the guy who I had just hours ago been given a no-contact order with. I felt like I was being set up. Although I knew this guy well, I hadn't seen him in a real long time and for all I knew he could have been snitching and trying to set me up so I didn't immediately talk to him. Eventually, I approached a random inmate on the tier and asked him if he would tell this guy, who I considered to be a friend, that I was just given a no-contact order with him at court today, but he didn't want to get involved.

He didn't know anything about us having a no-contact order because he wasn't at my court date, so it was weird that he didn't immediately come speak to me. That made it feel ever more like a set-up. However, it was awkward to be in such a close vicinity with someone I knew so eventually I said "fuck it" and approached him.

I let him know about the no-contact order and we chopped it up for a long time. He had been in the Pierce County Jail for around 9 months already at this time and was facing charges for the same bank scam that I was facing charges for. He was just one of many people I knew of who did the same thing as me but we didn't do it together and really had nothing to do with each other when it came to making money. He made the news as a ringleader so I guess they assumed that anyone in the area hitting bank licks that knew him must be part of his non-existent "identity theft ring".

Eventually my lawyer came by to see me and gave me my discovery that had all of the accusations against me as well as statements from people who had snitched on me and police reports related to my case. I had been snitched on by several people that had been paid a lot of money for me to use their bank card. Somehow, the police and the courts wanted to look at these people as victims. How are you a victim if you agree to commit a crime for financial purposes? I just don't understand it. One thing that most of them had in common was that they were white females. This country has a long history of racism and I guess they think that black males who do dirt with white females could only do so by force or coercion. The fact is that these people provided the most important element to hit a bank lick and that's their bank account. They did it to make money, knowing it was wrong, just as I did. They were my accomplices, not my victims.

It broke my heart to read the parts in the discovery regarding Theresa's interrogation. It was one thing when she told me that she told the truth when they presented her with evidence but seeing it on paper and seeing details about what was said made me mad. I felt like she was giving up information unnecessarily to get me in trouble and get herself out of trouble. I felt like I couldn't trust her at all. I was very happy that she didn't have any type of concrete information about other people besides me because she would have told anything she knew and that could have put her in danger.

She was shown a photo lineup of bank lick suspects and she told the detectives if and how she knew each person. Most of them were people she knew from school and she had never hit bank licks with any of them so she didn't have any information to give up about them. She told me they really wanted her to provide information about my friend I got placed in the same unit as but luckily for both her and him, she never did any dirt with him or witnessed him do any dirt, so she had nothing to tell.

After I got done with my lawyer I immediately shared my paperwork with my friend and he also shared his with me. I had never even been interrogated thanks to the fact that I came in with a paid lawyer so there was no way anyone was going to be able to accuse me of snitching. Unlike Theresa, I had a code to follow. Under no circumstance would I have given up information on someone else to get myself out of trouble. I was guilty, I committed these crimes, I was going to have suffer the consequences.

The next day after being placed in this unit I was called to roll up my stuff again. I was confused and I didn't know why because I figured I would be in that unit long-term. I assume that they caught on to the fact that I was placed in the same unit, on the same tier, as someone they had given me a no-contact order with. I wasn't happy at all to be getting moved because I liked the fact that I had someone I knew in there with me. However, it was out of my control and I was going somewhere else.

Once I got to the new unit I noticed that it was identical to the one I had just left. People were doing all the same things they were doing in the previous unit. I didn't realize it when I walked in but this unit would be the only room I see unless I was going to court for the next 8.5 months.

This time when I went to my bunk I was immediately greeted by my new bunk mate. Chuck was about 10-15 years older than I was and had spent plenty time in jail. I'm glad that I met somebody like him right away because if I didn't I probably would have just sat on my bunk doing nothing but he invited me to play chess.

Being in jail for the first time there are things you have to learn. For example, you don't want to take a shower without your shower shoes on. You don't want to sit on the toilet without covering it in toilet paper first. You have to be really careful not the catch MRSA. Having a veteran inmate like Chuck around helped me learn the dos and don'ts of being locked up.

My unit was full of cool people. Several other them I spent many months with. There were a lot of funny and interesting characters in there. I can truly say I made friends in there. Off the top of my head there was Fab, Damien, MC, HP, Top Dawg, Fresh, Cash, T-Loc, YL, Use, and a bunch of other people I was real cool with. I was often fascinated by the stories people would tell about what got them in trouble. I had deep conversations with a lot of different people.

When I first got to the county I had a little bit of money put on my books every now and then so I could buy snacks. I completely disregarded the fact that the judge gave me a no-contact order with Theresa so I would talk to her on the phone every day. We would end up arguing and she would hang up on me quite a bit just for me to call right back. Each call lasted 20 minutes and I would spend hours on the phone at a time. I also would sometimes have her make 3-way calls for people so I could get my hands on some extra commissary.

Chuck would always tell me that when you are doing time you have to let everything outside of those walls go because women tend to cheat on men who are gone for too long. He told me the worst thing I could do is argue with someone who is free while I am locked up. Although she had already proven she wasn't loyal to me I didn't really pay him too much attention when he said these things.

After being in the county jail for a little bit I became a regular gambler. I had Theresa give my lawyer my last $2,500 because I thought I still owed him money. I still to this day don't know if he was entitled to that $2,500 or just the retainer. I probably will never find out. Either way, we gave the lawyer our last so I wasn't able to have money put on my books any longer. If I wanted to get my hands on commissary, gambling was the way to do it.

Me and Chuck made a bet on pretty much every Sonics game that would come on, and also every Seahawks game. He was one of those people that always lived in Washington but hated all of the local sports teams. He also introduced me to poker and that became my favorite thing to do while I was locked up. I would play poker every single day. Each person would have to buy in with commissary adding up to one dollar and whether it was top ramen, envelopes, candy bars, or anything else we would let you in the game. I got pretty good and won quite a bit although I had never played the game before being locked up.

I also used to walk around the tier getting people to join in on a football pool where two top ramen would buy you 5 squares and if the score at the end of any quarter matched your square you would win 10 top ramens. Each paper had 100 squares, with each square representing two numbers. Let's say for example you had the square with 0 for the away team, and 6 for the home team. If the score at the end of the first quarter was 0 to 6, 10 to 6, 20 to 16, or any combination of scores in which the away team's last digit was 0 and the home team's last digit was 6, you would be the winner for that quarter. I absolutely loved doing this because it created excitement and anticipation for games that I otherwise might not have cared about. Sometimes the score would be the exact same or end in the same digits in back to back quarters so sometimes one football pool could feed me for a week.

People would gamble on any and everything in jail. A lot of us did it out of necessity, other people did it just to have something to do or because it was fun. There were many times when I had to fill out an indigent commissary slip and flip my two free envelopes into my food for the week. I absolutely refused to eat the breakfast food they served, hardly ever ate the lunch, and usually sold my dinner, so I relied heavily on gambling to prevent myself from starving.

While I was in the county jail the only time I left the unit was to go to court. I don't know if his is how it works in other counties but in Pierce County there is no such thing as a right to a speedy trial. Almost everyone who I ever spoke to about the subject was pressured by their own lawyer to sign away their right to a speedy trial. Their lawyer was usually a public defender who didn't really have their client's best interest at heart. They are often overworked so the continuances were in their own personal best interest. For the people who have their lives on the line, what's best is to have their constitutional right to a speedy trial respected. However, even if they refused to waive their rights the continuance would be forced because they were at the mercy of the courts. There were not a lot of people going to trial period and not one person who had their right to a speedy trial respected.

The people in control basically play a sick game with your life where you are chained up and walked to court just to have continuance after continuance asked for by both sides and granted by the judge. I personally felt like months and months were passing by without any progress being made. I was not being offered any sort of plea deals, my lawyer was telling me I was looking at decades in prison, and I was stuck with no options.

Eventually I got tired of my lawyer telling me I was looking at decades with no sort of details on how or why so I contacted the law library and got my hands on the sentencing guidelines. My highest charge was Identify Theft in the 1st degree and it was a charge I knew I would not be convicted of if I went to trial because I had not committed identify theft or even been involved in the bank lick that led to the charge. It made absolutely no sense to me when my lawyer told me that I am facing decades in prison so I had to find out for myself.

When I received the sentencing guidelines I learned that Identity Theft 1 carries a maximum of 84 months in prison. Seven years is still a long time but it wasn't decades like my lawyer had been telling me. Although I was a first-time offender, it became clear from the guidelines that when you are charged with multiple felonies it doesn't really matter. If you are a first timer with even 10 felony charges at one time you will be sentenced as if you had been in and out of prison nine times already.

A lot of people who grew up like me ended up becoming drug dealers. When you sell drugs you might get caught for selling to an undercover one time or you might get caught with drugs on you and get a possession or possession with intent to distribute charge. If this happens you will only be charged with that one time you were caught. However, when you hit bank licks, you might have done it way less times than the drug dealer has sold drugs, but they are able to max you out and give you the sentence of a life-long criminal who is a habitual recidivist. I don't see this as being fair at all but nothing about the criminal justice system is fair. It would be a major moral issue for me as both a prosecutor and as a judge if a 21-year-old who is in jail for the first time is being sentenced as if he had been in and out of prison nine times. Every first-timer who is charged with non-violent crimes should be given a second chance. If someone had been to prison four times for shooting someone, selling drugs, breaking into a house, and robbing someone, then came back on an Identity Theft 1 charge, they would have been looking at far less time than I was looking at my first time in jail. Is that what we call justice in America?

Once I got my hands on the sentencing guidelines I helped a lot of people figure out exactly how much time they were looking at. People would come to me regularly and I would ask how many prior convictions they had and could tell them the exact range that they would be sentenced to if found guilty of whatever felony they might be charged with. It seemed like most the people who I interacted with got offered plea deals which led to either less or lesser charges so I was telling them the worst-case which meant they would usually come back from their sentencing happy. Everyone who knew about my situation was blown away by the fact that I was charged with 30 felonies and assumed that the same would happen with me.

I went to hearing after hearing with no obvious progression with my case. At most of these so-called hearings I wouldn't ever see the judge, I would just talk to my lawyer for a short period and then be given paperwork. I felt like although I was presumed innocent until proven guilty that I was going to spend my whole life in jail going through the court process.

My original bail was set by one of those judges that no one wants to end up in front of. To be honest, my lawyer should have never had me turn myself in with her on the bench, but he did. I asked him to set up a bail reduction hearing for me with the hopes that a different judge might give me more credit for having no criminal record and turning myself in, but my request for a reduction was denied. It seemed to me like the judge just goes with whatever the prosecutor wants although I know that's not the case, at least it's not supposed to be. I could not make any sense out of having such a high bail for non-violent crimes when I turned myself in. This was not a murder case and I clearly was not running. I was not a threat to anyone. There is no way they can justify their decision outside of the fact that it's within their power to do whatever they want.

I was stuck, this was my life, and there was nothing I could do about it. As time went by I got more and more comfortable and being in jail became normal. I had a routine going and although time went by extremely slow, I was able to keep myself from going crazy or becoming completely miserable.

One of the things that made the time easier was the fact that I was locked up with so many cool people. One of the coolest people I met in there was this dude named Cash. At the time that we met I didn't know him but I knew who he was and I had been to a couple of his basketball games. Me and Cash used to chop it up all the time and one day we brought up the topic of no contact orders. We both had no contact orders issued with the mothers of our children. Neither one of us had seen our partners in life for quite some time.

We decided that we could get around the system if I signed his girl up for a visit and he signed up mine at the same time. The plan was for them to switch rooms when they got up there for the visit. We figured this was a good plan, and we were bold enough to try it, so we made a couple phone calls to set it up. In order to have a visitor come you are required to turn in a little yellow slip that has the visitor's information and the day and time that they will come. On my slip I wrote Cash's girl's information and I didn't have any second-thoughts or doubt that it would work. When it came to potential consequences for our visitors, we thought that the most that could happen is that these two women who can't visit us anyway would be banned from visiting. That might be the most that could happen to them, however, for me and Cash, if we were to get caught, it would surely be a new charge.

Despite the risk, we set up the visit for about three days out. Visits are only on specific days, and at specific times, based on your unit, so we didn't have many options. Our girls were both with it and available so we just had to wait for our names to get called when that day came.

At the Pierce County Jail the guards all have different styles and they conduct themselves differently. They all have different rules for what goes on in the unit. Some guards were straight assholes and wanted to make life as unpleasant as possible. Right when you see certain guards walk into the unit you already know what to expect.

There was this one guard that pretty much every inmate couldn't stand to see in the morning. This guard would come in and wake up every single person in the unit and have them make their bed nice and tight then force them to sit or stand in the day room as he went through this long spill about who he is and what his rules are. I personally looked forward to this shit because he mixed in humor and the man was hilarious. I couldn't help but laugh pretty much the whole time. It would be so funny when inmates would have to go through this for the first time because they would get pissed off and go through this tough guy act. I remember seeing one guy threaten to shoot him and get sent to the hole and he probably got a new charge too.

The guard's little speech he gave every morning was hilarious. A couple of the things he used to say that still stand out to me 10 years later is "If you don't like it, bail out." He would say that repeatedly after telling us a rule and the way he would say it would just have me cracking up laughing. Another thing he used to say is "I know a lot of you like to play dominoes, and you like to play cards, but please! Do not slam the dominoes or slap the cards on the table. A lot of you are in here for D.V. and it sounds like somebody is gettin their ass whooped. If you ever are gettin your ass whooped then yell out as loud as you can 'Help! Guard help!'". Even the so-called tough guys couldn't help but laugh a lot of the time.

To get back to why I brought him up, a couple days after we set up the visit he approached me on the tier.

"How you been youngster?" He asked.

"I'm good just trying to get this DOSA and get out of here." I responded.

"DOSA?"

"It's the drug offender sentencing alternative"

"You ain't no drug addict. I know a drug addict when I see one. What drugs you do?"

"A little bit of everything"

"Well, good luck with that. But let me tell you this, whatever it is you have planned tomorrow, don't do it."

"Huh? What are you talking about?"

"I was reading some notes in the computer and if I was you I wouldn't do what it is you are planning to do."

I was confused. Did they find out about the visit? They must have because what else could he be talking about.

"The last thing you want to do is catch a new case in the visiting room."

That confirmed it, they knew that we were trying to get around our no contact orders. We really should have known they would catch on. Sometimes when you are locked up you have to do what you have to do in order to stay sane. He wanted to see his girl and I wanted to see mine. To be honest the courts should never give two people with children a no contact order unless one party asks for it. Being co-defendants should never outweigh being co-parents. The courts prefer to terminate all contact between father and child although people in the United States who are accused of crimes are supposedly presumed innocent until proven guilty. What exactly does that mean if you can terminate a man's relationship with his children through a court order that says don't communicate with their mother? That is flat out evil and wrong. I believe they do it to intentionally destroy families and keep people trapped in the criminal justice system. Most people might think "why would they do that intentionally?" Well it damn sure isn't by accident and they definitely have no remorse.

I was extremely grateful for him warning me that they were going to catch us in the visiting room. He didn't have to do that, he could have just let us go through with it. I warned Cash and told him to tell his girl not to come and I told Theresa the same. Eventually, we set up a hearing to have the no-contact order between me and Theresa lifted and despite the prosecutor's evil objections the judge obliged and she was able to start visiting and bringing the kids to see me. My mom and sisters used to visit as well.

The rest of my time in the county jail was pretty much a whole bunch of doing the same thing, day after day. Watch sports, play poker, talk on the phone to Theresa, play chess, walk back and forth on the tier, and have conversations with the people I thought were cool.

My lawyer pretty much never had any information for me. My dad ended up calling him and cussing him out and he immediately came to visit me and I took it as a threat. I have no responsibility for my dad and I can't control what he does. Knowing my dad, I can only imagine how many times he called him a "white devil" and let him know that he is the "nigga of his nightmares". My dad didn't play any games when it came to the criminal justice system and he had a lot of experience and knowledge in that area. It was obvious to him and many other people that I wasn't quite being treated like someone who had paid $10,000 for services. I should have known more, and I should have known it sooner. I should have been presented with a plea deal.

I ended up spending 8 months in the county jail before my lawyer finally told me that I would have to plead guilty as charged or else the prosecutor would end up filing more charges against me and I would be given an exceptional sentence. Looking back, I don't believe that them adding more charges would have increased the amount of time that I was looking at and I don't think that my lawyer worked very hard for me. If he worked hard for me I'm not too sure what that work consisted of because there were no attempts made to actually fight my charges, even the ones I didn't do, and no plea deal was made. I won't claim that he spent no time at all on my case but I just don't know what he spent time doing.

12

GUILTY

On May 24th, 2007 I had to go in front of the judge to plead guilty. As far as I knew, this was the only way out of my situation because without pleading guilty I could end up waiting forever to go to trial. Going to trial could have possibly taken me years. Plus, I knew I was not innocent.

It was hard for me to accept the fact that once I plead guilty my sentence would be based on the one crime that I was charged with that I wasn't guilty of. If hitting bank licks required me to be an identity thief I would have had a lot more than one count of identity theft. The prosecutor was reaching and trying to increase the amount of time I would spend in prison and I still know for a fact that I would not have been found guilty of identity theft. I didn't have to steal anyone's identity in order to do what I was doing, that just wasn't a part of what I did.

Despite my reservations, despite the fear of what could happen when I was sentenced, I honestly felt like I had no choice but to plead guilty to every single charge. I wasn't presented with any other options. There was never any back and forth or negotiation. I was at the mercy of my lawyer and the prosecutor. Whatever went on between them behind closed doors, I had no knowledge of.

When I got in front of the judge I was extremely nervous. Whenever you plead guilty the judge asks a series of questions to make sure you understand what you are doing and that no one pressured you into your plea. I didn't fully understand why I was doing what I was doing at all and although no one pressured me I was led to believe that this was my best and only option. I informed the judge that the decision was made without coercion and my blank criminal history was instantly replaced by 30 new felony convictions.

This plea of guilty came along with a lot more than just jail time. I lost my right to vote and my right to carry a firearm in addition to losing my freedom. The 13th amendment abolished slavery but I also lost my right to not be enslaved as that amendment allows slavery as punishment for a crime. Everyone in prison gets put to work with serious consequences for refusing. My background would be forever tarnished. My options would be forever limited.

There was a 3 week wait in between my plea date and my sentencing date. I guess that is another part of the psychological war games that the criminal justice system plays with people. I don't see any reason why I couldn't be given my sentence immediately after pleading guilty but I guess that wouldn't have helped them in their attempts to break me down.

Within a matter of days after pleading guilty, a guard who was having a bad day kicked me out of the unit that I had spent the prior 8 months in. He told us we were not allowed to speak and I spoke so he decided to retaliate by attempting to lower my classification and risk level and having me shipped off to the old jail. I didn't disrespect the guy or do anything malicious but he was on a serious power trip that day. Luckily it was obvious to his superiors that he was taking his frustrations out on me and they over-rode his decision to move me to the old jail. I was sent to a new unit away from everyone I had gotten to know and basically had to start over while I waited to be sentenced.

In this new unit there were pretty much no poker players and there wasn't any action on sports either. I had nothing to do so I was bored out of my mind. I was also highly concerned about what was going to happen at my sentencing. This was probably the longest three weeks of my life.

On June 14th, 2007, the day had finally arrived when I would learn my fate. I couldn't sleep at all the night before. All I could think about was my son and how old he might be by the time I was released. Would he even want anything to do with me? Would I be sent far away where he could never visit? Would he even remember me? I assumed that no matter what Theresa and Nariya wouldn't be around waiting for me. Theresa had visited not long after I plead guilty and informed me that she was seeing other people, so although I wouldn't expect her to allow me to continue a relationship with her daughter I fully expected to be a part of my son's life.

I went through the process that had become so familiar in which I got chained to a bunch of other inmates and walked through the long and cold hallways from the jailhouse to the courthouse. I wanted to stay calm and relaxed but although my mind wanted to remain calm, my body was anxious.

As I sat and waited for my turn in front of the judge, I was listening to two guys who also had court that day talk. They were dressed in orange and shackled which meant they were in the hole. They were the suspects in a double murder and one of them was so crazy that he was saying he wanted to get "fuck my victim" tattooed on his face. He didn't seem to care who knew he was guilty despite the fact that they were fighting for their lives. He was saying that he hoped he got the death penalty as they were facing a capital murder case. As I listened to them and looked around I began to feel more confident about my chances. I knew I wasn't like them. The same judge who would be sentencing me had also dealt with real life monsters and hitting bank licks was nothing compared to taking a life. I had no priors, this was my first time ever in jail and I had already been here for a long time, maybe I would be given a second chance and an opportunity to prove that my criminal lifestyle was behind me.

Once it was my turn to get in front of the judge, I really just didn't want to go. I wished that I could just skip through the whole dog and pony show and get down to the consequences for my actions. My lawyer had talked to me ahead of time and told me what to expect and I didn't really want any part of this pre-scripted game that is played with people's lives.

The way the sentencing hearing is set up the prosecutor got to talk first, followed by my lawyer, and then the prosecutor again before the judge makes his decision. When the prosecutor opened up I was made to look more evil and bad than you could ever imagine. Unsubstantiated claims flew around left and right. This person who did not know me and never got a chance to speak to me had and idea made up in their mind of who I was and they couldn't have possibly been further from the truth. Just as my lawyer had warned me, the prosecutor recommended that I serve the maximum, 84 months, or 7 years, in prison. They didn't care that this was my first time in jail, they didn't care about my young age, and they didn't care that I had a young child. Sentencing ranges exist for a reason, the maximum is reserved for the worst of the worst. To the prosecutor, I guess that's who I was.

When my lawyer got a chance to speak he earned every penny that I had paid him. I'm not too sure how much work he had done for me up until that point but his performance in the courtroom that day was amazing. The unfortunate part is that the picture he painted of me was just as inaccurate as the picture that the prosecutor had painted of me. The way the criminal justice system works, truth does not really matter much. Both sides have a story to tell and the truth is usually somewhere in the middle, if anywhere to be found. My lawyer told the judge that I did not have nice things or live a life of luxury and that every penny I made went on drugs, which then went up my nose. Although I had never done cocaine a day in my life it was his job that day to make the judge believe I was a cocaine addict who should receive the drug offender sentencing alternative. While many people think that drug offender sentencing is only for people with drug charges that is not the case, it is for drug addicts.

My lawyer got extremely animated and spoke in a way that I can do no justice here in the pages of this books. He appeared to get so angry and began to chastise the judge about a perceived lack of awareness of sentencing alternatives when judges make sentencing decisions. He wanted to make it plain and clear to the judge that there were alternatives to sentencing me within the standard range, and especially at the high-end of it as the prosecutor wanted.

When the prosecutor got the chance to speak again it was pretty much more of the same, an attempt to make me look as bad as possible. I don't really know how the prosecutor justified to herself asking for the maximum sentence for a first-timer but she had it in her head that I deserved it.

Right before the judge made his decision I was given a chance to speak. My lawyer had told me ahead of time that if I choose to speak I should make sure that I am apologetic and make no attempts to excuse my behavior. I made sure to apologize and stick to the script although I had a lot more to say.

The judge looked me in my eye and asked my age. I told him that I was 22 years-old. He said that since I was so young he was going to give me a break and give me the drug offender sentencing alternative. However, he followed that by saying he was also going to go also go with the prosecutor's recommendation of the maximum sentence. When he said this everyone involved was confused including me, my attorney, and the prosecutor. What the judge had just said made no sense.

When someone is sentenced under the drug offender sentencing alternative, they are required to serve half of the mid-range for their offense. My highest charge, as previously mentioned, was Identify Theft in the 1st degree. Since I would be sentenced as if I already had 9 previous felony convictions, my standard range was between 63 and 84 months. Therefore, if I received the drug offender sentencing alternative my sentence would be half of 73 months which is 36.5 months. The additional half would be served on community supervision, aka probation.

After a short period of confusion, the prosecutor informed the judge that he would not be able to impose a sentence that agreed with both sides. He would have to sentence me to either the drug offender sentencing alternative or the high end of the standard range, both was not an option. If the judge had his way my sentence would have been 42 months of incarceration with 42 months of probation and that is a lot closer to siding with us over siding with the prosecutor who wanted me to serve 84 months in prison. The judge informed the prosecutor that he was still going to go with the drug offender sentencing alternative and I looked back at my family with a huge smile on my face, feeling relieved.

I considered this outcome to be a win. Although I was headed to prison, which was a scary thought, I would be free by 2008 which was the next year. When I walked into that room there was a possibility that I was going to do a lot more time than that so I couldn't do anything but be happy. I didn't fully grasp at the time what it meant to be sentenced under the drug offender sentencing alternative but it cut my time in half and that was something I was grateful for.

I spent the next five days thinking about what prison might be like while I waited to be sent to Washington Corrections Center in Shelton, which is the receiving institution for the Washington State Department of Corrections. Every male who goes to prison in the state of Washington has to go to Shelton first. I didn't know what it was going to be like once I got there but a lot of people in the county jail who had been to prison talked about it as if it were hell. They would always say that doing time in prison is much easier and much better than doing time in the county but they said the R-Units at Washington Corrections Center are the worst part of being locked up, period.

On June 19th, 2007, I was called for the final time at the Pierce County Jail to roll up. I gave away anything that might have had value such as snacks or envelopes and packed everything else. I didn't know at the time but I was about to go through the most degrading experience that I would ever have to go through in my life.

Everyone who is being sent to Washington Corrections Center in Shelton is gathered up and taken in to a concrete room with a bench attached to the wall. We are forced to all stand up on the bench and one by one get down, strip naked, bend over, cough, and lift our ball sack. You can tell that some of the people had been through this before and it was nothing for them to go through this. However, for me, I felt completely violated. I didn't believe it was necessary to make grown men strip naked in front of each other and expose themselves. While they pretend that they are doing this to make sure that no one brings contraband with them from the jail to the prison, it is another method used to break you down. I felt like they were exerting their will and letting us know that they were the bosses and we were no longer in control of our lives.

Once we went through this degrading process we were put on a bus and the journey to Shelton began. After being stuck in the same building and not seeing outside for 8.5 months I was pretty excited to go on the bus ride. I enjoyed riding through Tacoma and seeing familiar buildings that I hadn't seen in so long. I enjoyed seeing people who were free moving about and living their lives. I was very happy to be outside of those walls.

Although I was happy to be leaving one building, I was nervous and worried about the one I was headed to. Whatever nervousness I had about going to jail for the first time was multiplied by 10,000 when it came to going to prison for the first time. While I was in the county I asked the veterans who had been in and out of jail and prison their whole life a lot of questions about the process and what prison was like. Each person had a different experience and a difference perspective so although I was able to learn some things about what I should expect it still wasn't quite clear.

On the way to Shelton we stopped at multiple other county jails to pick people up. They put everyone on the same bus whether they are headed to prison to serve a 30-day probation violation or if they are headed to spend the rest of their life in prison. They don't care if you are there for a non-violent crime or a murder, we all got treated the same.

When we finally approached the prison it looked like something out of the movies or a TV show. The barbed wire around the extremely tall fences and the gun towers coming into my line of sight led to extreme nervousness. I was actually here. I was actually pulling up to a prison and there was absolutely nothing I could do in order to get myself out of this situation.

When we got inside of the prison we had several tasks to complete. We had to have a mental health evaluation, we had to have our physical health evaluated, we had to fill out paperwork, we had to be issued our clothing, and we had to have our picture taken and be issued our prison identification. This whole process took hours to complete. We had left the Pierce County Jail early in the morning but it wasn't until the late afternoon when we finally reached our cells.

When I made it to the tier I was once again reminded of something from television. The receiving units were just like what I had previously seen on TV. There were two floors, with probably 15 2-man cells on each floor. There were people shouting and making a lot of noise. Each cell had a bunk bed and a toilet with a sink attached. This was nothing like the county jail that I had just left with the open tiers and the big open day room. We had bars, just like on TV. We were in cages like animals.

Everyone there had yet to be classified. It was very possible to have a 30-day probation violator sharing a cell with a murderer who was going to spend the rest of their life in prison. I got lucky, my cellmate was an 18-year-old who I had been in the Pierce County Jail with. Although he had served time in a juvenile prison this was his first time in the adult prison. He was in prison for a gun charge but was only going to serve less than a year before being released. His baby-face and long hair had him a little worried about having to prove he wasn't soft.

We used to talk about any and everything to kill the time. He was a pretty funny guy and had an affinity for pirates, especially Captain Jack Sparrow from the Pirates of the Caribbean movies. I can still picture him standing on one leg doing his best Johnny Depp impression. I have to say I was extremely grateful for ending up in a cell with him because it could have been so much worse.

I didn't take having a cool celly for granted. I knew it was only a matter of time before I would be uprooted and have to start all over. When you first get to the Washington Corrections Center you are placed in the lower R-units until you are classified. Once you are classified you are moved to the upper R-units, with the exact unit determined by your classification level. Although not all people in prison are horrible people I would assume that there are more people who I'd rather not share a cell with than those who I would want to share with. Unfortunately, I didn't have a choice.

13
DOING TIME

My first few weeks in prison were actually not that bad compared to the 8.5 months I spent in the county jail. I was happy to have better food. I was happy to have the opportunity to go outside and walk the yard. I was happy to have the opportunity to play sports. I was happy to have the opportunity to not be stuck inside of the same room for weeks at a time. It felt amazing to go outside and breathe fresh air and have sunlight hit my body. I was surprised to find out that there was a movie night where we got to watch a new movie that was newly released on DVD. I learned quickly that being in prison gave you a lot more liberties than being in the county jail.

Despite having more liberties than being in the county, I was still in prison and this was not the place to be. Things definitely could get worse for me. Something as simple as getting a different celly could change my entire experience. The guy in the cell next door always had crazy stories to tell and I could have ended up with someone like him. He most likely had mental health issues. He had spent a lot of time in the hole while he was in the county and told us about throwing his shit and piss at the guards. He was one of those guys that talked real tough and didn't take any shit from the guards because he didn't mind being in isolation. It almost seemed like he wanted to go to the hole. I would not have felt comfortable sharing such a small space with this guy. Ironically, I ran into to him once we were both free and he seemed perfectly normal. The effects of prolonged isolation must have worn off.

Being out on the yard made me nervous at first but eventually I was able to just soak it in and enjoy it. The weather was nice in Shelton in the Summer and I really looked forward to yard time after being trapped indoors for so long. I had yard in the lower R-units at the same time as someone I knew so I walked around with him talking about old times. I also ran in to someone I didn't know very well but had seen around and had a couple of conversations with. I spent time hanging with him on the yard as well.

I didn't know anything about being in prison but I had heard stories so I was always extremely cautious. It seemed like every single day fights would break out on the yard and more often than not it was due to gang activity. It seemed like every time a Norteño or Sureño laid eyes on one of their rivals they had to immediately throw down. There was a stabbing on the yard while I was there and I probably saw at least 10 fights between members of those two Mexican gangs. I had a lot to learn about prison politics and how to avoid conflict.

The group of people I was on the yard with at any given time was as diverse as you could imagine. The people on the yard ranged from under 18 years old to senior citizens. There were people of every ethnicity. There were people being released within the month as well as people who would never be released. There were car thieves and murderers. People who wrote bad checks and people who had stabbed or shot multiple people. People who smoked weed and had their probation violated and people who manufactured meth and blew up buildings. No matter who you were, no matter your circumstances, we all ended up right here in the same place.

Three weeks after I arrived in Shelton, I had settled in. I had gotten used to being inmate #305986. This was my reality and in honesty it wasn't all that bad compared to my fears and expectations. Me and my celly got along great, I had come across a couple people who I knew from the streets, I was beginning to get used to my daily routine. Unfortunately, it was about to be time to start all over.

The classification process was over for me after three weeks in the lower R-units and it was time for me to go to the upper R-units. The upper R-units were my final stop at the Washington Corrections Center as I waited to be sent to the institution where I would serve out my sentence. There was no pre-determined amount of time that I would spend in Shelton so I had no idea how long I would be there. All I knew was that I had been classified and I was being moved to R-4.

When I got to the upper-Rs I was relieved to see that I was no longer in a place that resembled the movies. There were no more bars. There was only one floor. I still had to shower side-by-side with other men but it was obvious that my routine and experience was about to be a little bit different. Although I was classified as minimum security, I went from maximum security in the lower-Rs to medium security in the upper-Rs and that allowed for more movements and less restriction.

When I got to my cell I was greeted by my new celly who was from Samoa. He was soft-spoken and seemed pretty chill so I was relieved. My sister Sareeta has children with two Samoan men and my celly said he knew one of them. Ironically, the other one, the father of her oldest, was in the upper R-units at the same time as me and I ran into him a few times. Once it was during a visit when my mom and my sister, Nikki, came to see me so they got to see him too. This is the same guy who used to live with us. The same guy whose check I stole when I first headed down this path of destruction involving bank licks and bad checks.

After a couple days, my celly got moved out and sent to his institution. That same day, a new celly moved in. This time it was a white guy. He didn't appear to be a white supremacist, but then again a lot of people who turn into white supremacist in prison come in looking just like him. He seemed nervous when he entered our cell but I introduced myself anyway, after that he made his bunk and began to read his Bible.

I spent pretty much all of my time in the cell reading. I had checked out a book called "Left Behind" which was about the Rapture which is when all people who are saved by Christ disappear off the Earth and this group of people called the Tribulation Force go through all kinds of stuff trying to survive and defeat the anti-Christ. Once I finished that first book I learned that there were a lot more in the series so I read them all. These were not short books at all but with me being trapped in a cell I could read a whole book in a day or two easily.

Once my celly noticed what I was reading he asked me if I wanted to pray with him. I did it and from that point we began to talk more and even play Yahtzee with dice he made out of toilet paper and toothpaste. He seemed like a pretty normal and decent guy. Through our conversations it had come up multiple times what I was in prison for but I began to notice that he never once spoke on why he was in there.

One day I was coming back from eating and I had another inmate approach me asking questions about my celly. He told me that my celly was a sex offender and that I needed to check him. When you first get to prison you are informed that doing anything to a sex-offender will get you charged with a hate crime. I told him that what my celly was in there for had nothing to do with me and I was trying to get home as soon as possible. He told me to be careful because when you are cellys with a chimo (prison slang for child molester) and you don't do anything about it, you can easily be placed on the same level and end up with a target on your back.

This was my worst nightmare. For one, I wasn't comfortable sharing a small space with a child molester. This man had seen pictures of my children. I was pissed off and nervous at the same time because I knew I was stuck. I was not going to jeopardize catching a new charge or doing anything to this guy. At the same time, I did not want to be in the cell with him. I decided I was going to talk to him and see if it was true and take it from there.

Once we were both back in the cell I asked my celly what he was in prison for. He looked at me very nervously and admitted to being a sex offender. He told me that he had moved away from home for a while and when he came back he fell in love with his younger sister. He claims they had a mutual sexual relationship but he was grown and she was a minor and on top of that they were blood brother and sister. He was in prison for incest and statutory rape.

Apparently, we both had the same lawyer for our cases. This man originally was given no jail time and had certain conditions he had to meet in order to stay free under a special sex-offender sentencing alternative. He violated those conditions by leaving the state with his victim and that is what led to him being in prison and sharing a cell with me.

I was disgusted by what I had heard. I was not just disgusted with this man's actions but I was also disgusted by the fact that I was sent directly to prison while he received a slap on the wrist and had to mess up again before being sent here. Is statutory rape and incest not more serious than writing bad checks? Was this man seriously not considered more of a threat than I was?

I told him that what he did was between him and God and that although I wasn't cool with it, and didn't condone it, I wasn't going to do him any harm. I warned him that other people in our unit knew that he was a sex-offender and that he might not be safe there. He responded with a verse from the Bible and made it clear that he wasn't going to write a kite asking to be moved so I left it at that.

I couldn't help but notice that the inmates here are not considered human beings by anyone involved in the criminal justice system. There is absolutely no regard for us. From day one when I walked into that courtroom I was treated as less than human. They attempted to cut off communication between me and my family, they locked me in a cage indefinitely with an impossible bail, they attempted to give me the maximum sentence allowable, then on top of that they sent me to be with rapist and murderers who they would never themselves want to share a room with.

I feel like every police officer, judge, defense attorney, prosecutor, and corrections officer should have to go through these experiences themselves before being considered qualified to make decisions about other people's lives. How can any decent or moral person play a role in sending someone from a disadvantaged background who wrote bad checks to share space with rapist and murderers? How could they justify placing me on the same level and in the same place as people who have acted violently and with no regard for other human beings? How can they send a probation violator whose only crime is being a drug addict to this same place with someone who shot four people and will be serving 40 years? How do they end up sharing a cell? I don't know how any players of the criminal justice game can sleep at night. There are even innocent people who they have sent to these places. It is completely un-justifiable. Not every crime should be punishable by imprisonment and you should at least be around people who committed similar crimes.

Luckily for me, I was classified into minimum security. After a few weeks in the upper R-units I was sent on a bus to Larch Corrections Center in Yacolt, Washington. I got a completely different vibe pulling up to Larch than I did when I pulled up to Washington Corrections Center. This place didn't look like a prison at all. There were no gun towers. There was a gate but it was nothing like the gates in Shelton.

Larch was not a very big institution and it looked more like an apartment complex to me than a prison. It didn't take long once I got there for me to realize that where I had just left was the penitentiary, where I was now, was a camp. The intake process was also a lot faster. After a short while I was given a tan jacket, a couple pairs of tan jeans, a couple red shirts, and a pair of black velcro shoes to wear and sent to my unit.

At Larch, there are no controlled movements for the general population. There was a library, a gym and a yard just like at Washington Corrections Center but here we had a lot more opportunity to utilize them. Inside the gym I was surprised to see a rec room with pool tables, ping-pong tables, and dart boards. The tiers are all open and lined with cubicles. Inside of each cubicle there was a table and two beds.

After I got settled in I was happy to run into someone I knew. He gave me some top ramen, candy bars, snacks, and essentials such as soap and toothpaste. He also told me all about serving time at Larch. He warned me that since I was on a drug offender sentence I would most likely leave general population and be placed into a drug treatment/behavior modification program called Integrity.

My first day at Larch I caught a glimpse of the segregation within the prison system. At Washington Corrections Center, inmates have no choice about where they sit down to eat and who they sit with. There, your seat is determined by your place in line. However, at Larch there is more open movement and you don't have to line up to walk to the chow hall. You know when it's time to eat so you show up and you sit in your spot. Everyone at the institution has a specific table and seat where they eat, however, it is not assigned. You will not find many black people sitting at the table with white people. You will not find people from rival gangs sitting at the same table.

In prison, who you eat with is very important because that's the group you are lumped into. Black people eat with black people. White people eat with white people. Mexican people eat with Mexican people. Sex offenders eat with sex offenders. White supremacist eat with white supremacist. Crips eat with Crips. GDs eat with GDs.

If you are like me and not associated with or lumped in to any certain group that can lead to trouble in the chow hall. Although we were in minimum security, sitting in the wrong place can lead to a fight with the quickness. When I walked into the chow hall for the first time I began scanning the room trying to figure out where I could sit and I was relieved to be waved down by my homeboy who is from the Central District. The majority of the people who sat at his table were from Union and they all knew members of my family from being born and raised in the Central District. Although I wasn't from Union that was still the best place for me to sit and eat.

After finally settling in at Larch, it was time for another shakeup. My friend's prediction that I would be pulled out of general population and into the Integrity program came true. I had to exchange my red shirts for burgundy and move to a different area of the Elk Horn building. Members of the Integrity program were required to be separated from the general population because they lived by different rules. While everyone at Larch was required to work and pretty much got to move freely outside of work, in the Integrity program, you had to line up for most movements and you had to go to all kinds of meetings and classes outside of work.

Almost everyone who had warned me about the possibility of entering the Integrity program told me that in this program the inmates are forced to snitch on each other. Whenever someone violates a rule you are supposed to "raise their awareness" by approaching them, telling them what they did wrong, and dropping a piece of paper in a box telling on them so they could face consequences. This was something that I was worried about because there was no way I could participate in that. What could they possibly be thinking when they decided that they should have convicts who are serving time in prison snitch on each other? Everybody dreaded having to enter the program for this reason. A lot of people decided that they weren't going to do it and got cuffed up and sent out of the institution on a 557, which is a major infraction for failure to program. Some people were willing to lose their drug offender sentencing over it which would essentially double their time in prison.

Once you enter the Integrity program the whole concept of doing time changes. For a lot of people, that change is for the better. The program is designed to get people thinking about their self-destructive behaviors and replacing them with more positive behaviors. The program is designed to be one year long and inmates hit milestones and progress in stages as they complete each step of the program. While there is a heavy focus on drug addiction and that is the key problem being addressed, the curriculum allows people to think about and work toward changing all self-destructive behavior that leads to incarceration. I felt like I personally did not need this program but I definitely needed half of my time knocked off. If I was going to succeed I was going to have to pretend to be someone who I wasn't.

14
INTEGRITY

When you enter drug treatment, the treatment providers want to see progress. You cannot successfully complete drug treatment if you claim to not have a problem. One of the first steps to getting better for people who are truly in addiction is admitting that they have a problem. I was diagnosed as being addicted to cocaine despite the fact that I had never tried cocaine. If I came into this program telling them that I don't use drugs that would not have gotten me anywhere. Once I was diagnosed there was no way they would even believe me. It was in my best interest to take on the role of a cocaine addict and use that as my material for going through treatment. We would have to write about and talk about our problems so I had to get myself into character despite not even knowing how much cocaine someone might do at one time or how it makes you feel.

The first thing they do for new people in the program is assign them a "big brother". This big brother is supposed to show you the ropes of the program and get you through phase one and into phase two where you can be more independent. While in phase one you have to sit by your big brother when you eat and in meetings. This meant that all of the prison politics was out the window in the Integrity program, at least during phase one. My big brother was a white guy who was in the program because of a meth addiction. We didn't really have anything in common but he did a good job teaching me about the program. He even taught me the way around having to snitch on people while in the program which was to make trades. He let me raise his awareness about something small and bogus one day, then a little while later I would return the favor.

The meetings in this program were sometimes entertaining but mostly a bunch of bullshit. I can't tell you how many times the behavior of a couple people got us all pulled into these long meetings and chastised. Somehow the people in charge didn't realize that chastising people who had nothing to do with what happened is not a good way to solve a problem. We were supposed to be a community, and in their world of make-believe, we were all responsible for each other. This meant they would punish us all whenever something major happened. For example, there was a string of thefts in the kitchen and although there were only a couple people stealing we were all required to sit and be chastised about it and forced to try to come up with solutions.

When you do something against the rules, for example, cussing, you have to go in front of one of the counselors and your peers to either dispute that you committed the act or receive your punishment. Punishments come in many forms. You might have to hold the door for everyone while repeating "I will show respect", or something along those lines, depending on what you did. You might be required to write and act out a skit in front of the group. You might be required to sing a song. You might be required to write a short paper. If you committed a violation of the rules that was also a major infraction that was the only time you would face serious consequences. All other consequences were simply to help you think about and learn from whatever happened. For people who actually buy in and want to be held accountable this is a great idea, however, for the majority of people who were forced against their will to enter this program, this is a horrible idea.

Despite the minor consequences, I still didn't think it was ok to have inmates policing other inmates. If everyone completely bought in to the program then that could work, however, since not everyone buys in it can lead to people getting hurt. I saw multiple fights occur over one inmate raising another inmate's awareness. Even when the offense is petty you are still observing someone doing something and telling the authorities. In prison, and on the streets, that is unacceptable when you live by "the code".

As I progressed in the program I formed a tight circle of friends. At our table there was Ray, Torri, Angelo, Bryan and Leon. Ray and Torri were cousins. Ray was a Crip from Hilltop in Tacoma, Torri was a little bit older and from Everette, Angelo was a GD from Bremerton, Bryan was a little older and from Tacoma, and Leon was a half-white Mexican from Centralia who went from hanging with the white supremacist to hanging with us. Our little group formed naturally and we all looked out for each other and shared with each other. We also would all take turns dropping papers on each other so it looked like we were participating in raising people's awareness so that we could progress through the stages of the program.

Although we were all cool, every now and then we would get into it with each other. One time Torri legitimately raised my awareness and I went back to sit with my big brother for like a week before they finally convinced me to come back to the table. I had no respect for that because it just wasn't something that we did. Besides that, it was mostly all fun and games, we spent a lot of time laughing and joking around.

I was close to all of these guys but I probably had the most in common with Angelo. We both were on all the sports teams when the seasons came up. We played basketball, volleyball, and kickball. We were partners in all of the pool and dart tournaments, which we won a couple of. When we weren't teammates we were always competing.

Angelo was one of those people who was in prison for a long time but didn't deserve to be. He was serving a five-year sentence for burglary without actually being a burglar. It was one of those cases where the laws are written poorly and prosecutors can stretch the facts into a much more major conviction than what should have taken place.

Apprently, Angelo and the mother of his child had a no-contact order after a domestic violence situation. While I have no sympathy for domestic abusers and men who are violent toward women, not everyone who ends up arrested for domestic violence and issued a no-contact order is a bad guy. The criminal justice system does not require much to take place in order for this to happen. You don't have to harm anyone or intend harm to anyone in order for an arrest to happen and a no-contact order to be issued.

Unfortunately, many of the parties to no-contact orders have very strong feelings toward one another and rely on each other. When this is the case, no-contact orders will be broken. Often, it is the victim that makes first contact and tries to persuade the other person to come back home. When that person comes back home, it is not both people who are risking a new charge, just the person who got arrested and issued the no-contact order. This creates situations in which both parties can be equally guilty in regards to violating a no-contact order but only one of them will be subject to consequences.

When Angelo returned home after receiving a no-contact order, everything was all good and the relationship got back to normal. Eventually he got in a non-violent argument with his girl and she told him to leave. They lived together and they both had all of their possessions in their home. Angelo left when he was told but he figured that after there was time for them to calm down he would go back home. When he got home he knocked on the door and his girl wouldn't answer. He didn't have a key so he climbed in the window. When he got inside his girl was in there with another man and Angelo grabbed some stuff and left without confrontation. His girl was ashamed of herself and worried that Angelo might try to take their son so she called the police on him and he was arrested. He was arrested for violation of a no-contact order and burglary. Was Angelo completely innocent in this situation? Of course not. Did he deserve to spend five years in prison? Hell no. His girl's actions were due, in part, to the fact that she was cheating on him. She was also just as guilty as he was in regards to him violating the no-contact order to begin with.

Despite this being Angelo's home he was charged with burglary because by definition you commit burglary when you enter a building unlawfully with the intent to commit a crime. They say the crime he intended to commit was violation of a no-contact order. Angelo definitely could have been lying to me but I have seen these situations occur all too often. I don't know many young black males who have not at some point been in a situation that could have gotten them arrested for domestic violence and many of them did no harm. I also know others who did a lot of harm and deserved everything they got and then some.

Outside of the people that I ate with and hung with the most, there were a lot of other cool people in the Integrity program. I was on the tier one day telling a story about hitting bank licks and this older guy named Mike Jones thought I was full of shit and told me he would have robbed me. We got in an argument but eventually it came out that he was my aunties ex-boyfriend and he knew my mom, my dad and my whole family. He ended up being someone I was real cool with. He told me stories about how him, my aunt, my dad and other family members ran an after-hours spot where people would come to get high, eat food and get drunk once bars were closed back in the day.

When I came into the program there was a Mexican guy named Garza who came in with me at the same time. We were tight just because we had to learn the ropes together. He also liked to gamble so we spent a lot of time playing poker and a game called casino.

There was a guy named Riggins who finished the program right as I was coming in but he was real cool too. He gave me a pair of Chuck Taylor's when he was released. There was also a guy named Ted who knew a lot of my family. He ended up being the President of the program. He used to look out for me and try to get me to work out.

My time in the Integrity program gave me an opportunity to think long and hard about my future. Although I was completing what was considered to be intensive in-patient drug treatment, the value for me was in the behavior modification aspects. We were forced to look at what we wanted to do with our lives once that release date came. A lot of the people in the program had been in and out of prison many times and although they said they had enough they often spoke about the reality of getting out and having nothing. It's rare to be released from prison after serving a long sentence and have clothes to wear, a car to drive, and even food to eat. A lot of the old vets who had been through this many times talked about how they got out of prison intending to stay out and do right but their circumstances just wouldn't allow it. It's hard to find a job, it's hard to find a place to live, it's hard to find an opportunity.

How can anyone expect you to get out, do better, and turn your life around if you can't make an honest living or find a place to call home? I remember being in one of the classes for the Integrity program and the counselor and everyone in my group made staying out of prison sound impossible. I told them that I would sign up for food stamps, I could find housing, and utilize other resources out there but they repeatedly shut down anything I said and basically told me that it's not going to happen like that once I got out. I got so angry that I stood up and cussed out everyone in the room and basically told them that they are the sources of their own problems and that I was not like them and I was going to succeed no matter what. Despite my blow up, which violated numerous rules, the counselor didn't even attempt to punish me. She had to know that I was right. The doom and gloom attitude was a major problem and as a counselor she should have never helped contribute to it.

While I was at Larch I got occasional visits from my Mom, my sisters, Theresa and the kids. Theresa was still going through the motions in her own court case. She was arrested before me but I went through my whole case and had been sent to prison with her still out on bail. It made absolutely no sense to me.

I received mail from a very good friend of mine named Jason but that was the only person I hung with, including my cousins, that I heard from the whole time I was locked up. A lot of my homeboys and cousins also hit bank licks so I wasn't surprised that I didn't hear from them. I probably would have been cautious about that as well. Eventually, me and Theresa had stopped talking completely. For a while I completely lost contact with the outside world, and that was probably a good thing.

I didn't know it at the time but my family was going through it. My dad had lost his place to live and was back to being a transient. My mom, Nikki, and my step-dad Fred were in and out of the hospital with health problems related to diabetes and other conditions they were battling. Sareeta had given up her kids to their dads and started living a very unhealthy lifestyle for a period of time. I got word through another inmate that my cousins Jay and Mak had beef with each other and Mak had gotten shot several times in an attempted robbery in Arizona. I felt like I might have been in the best shape out of most of the people I was close to despite the fact that I was in prison. At least Mo was doing good, he was playing professional basketball in Portugal and had also spent time playing for the Harlem Globetrotters. I didn't hear from him the whole time I was locked up due to him being out of the country and on the move.

As I was getting ready to hit phase three of the Integrity program I was called in to talk to a classification officer. Apparently, there had been a mistake made in regards to my release date and good time. They had me scheduled to be released in August but my actual release date was in June. I was so pumped about this. I was going to be free in time for Summer meaning the only Summer I would have spent locked up is Summer 2007.

When I got the news that I would be released sooner than expected, the people who ran the Integrity program decided to let me do phase three and phase four at the same time. If I didn't do it this way I wasn't going to finish. Due to my drug offender sentencing, long-term treatment was something that would be required of me whether I did it on the inside or the outside of prison and I did not want to have to start all over once I was released. I was given a special exception to the rule that requires all inmates to work and relieved from my duties in the kitchen so that I could focus on doubling up my classes and meetings so that I could finish the program before my release date.

In addition to finishing the Integrity program I also had to figure out whose house I was going to release to. In the state of Washington when you have court ordered probation, if your release date comes and you do not have an approved address to release to, you stay in prison. You have to go through a process in which you submit the address you will release to and someone representing the Department of Corrections has to go out and inspect the place. What they are looking for during this inspection, I don't know. In my opinion, if that release date has come, people should be set free, but who am I? As a convicted felon I was not going to be able to live with anyone who lived in an apartment complex because most apartments don't allow people with felony convictions. My only option was to get back in touch with Theresa and try to release to her mom's house. Theresa's mom was the only person I knew in Pierce County who owned a home and wouldn't have to deal with problems from a landlord due to having a felon living there.

I wrote Theresa and despite the fact that we hadn't spoken in a long time, she got her mom to agree to let me release to their house. This was something that I didn't want to do but I didn't have any options. In my mind, Theresa had abandoned me and I didn't feel like our relationship was repairable, but I had to do what I had to do.

Once I had a clear path to my release, the rest of my time at Larch went pretty smoothly. Well, almost. I had a medical situation where I felt extremely sick and had to be excused from regular programming and lie in bed all day. Once night hit I felt like I was going to die and I struggled to get up and make my way to the guard's station. I was on the lower floor and when I got to the guard's station no one was there. I struggled to walk up the stairs and right when I got to the upper-level guard's desk I collapsed. I'm not too sure how long I was lying there but I woke up confused. I had a few inmates standing over me asking if I was ok. Apparently, after I collapsed the first time, I tried to get up and collapsed again. I had no recollection of getting up and passing out a second time. Eventually, the guards came and escorted me to a room in the institution where I sat and received no medical attention. After a while I was given some water and eventually sent back to my bunk. I have no idea what was wrong with me but with the lack of medical attention I am glad that it couldn't have been anything too serious.

Outside of that scary situation, it was smooth sailing. Once I got news that my time would be cut short and I was able to stop working in the kitchen doing time was easy. Completing two phases of the Integrity program at once kept me busy at all times. The more you have to do, the faster time appears to go by. Before I knew it, my release date had come.

The night before my release from prison I couldn't sleep at all. I was very excited, anxious and scared all at the same time. I didn't know what the future held for me. I didn't know where my next dollar would come from. I didn't know what I was going to do with myself. The one thing I knew for sure was that once I walked out of that gate, I never planned on coming back.

The morning of my release I had to go around getting documents signed from various people within the institution, then I had to turn in all of my state issued clothing besides what I had on, along with my bedding. I gave away everything I had of value, besides my radio. That radio costs hundreds of dollars once they take out all of the deductions from money that gets sent to you. A lot of people wanted it but I was worried about getting in trouble since my DOC number was engraved in it. Looking back, I was just paranoid and should have left the radio for one of my homeboys, they weren't going to find it and keep me there.

Once my ride arrived, I was given clothes to change into and I got out of the state issued prison gear. All that was left was for me to receive my $40 check and then they would pop that gate and let me out. I was given an envelope with my probation paperwork and told to check in with probation within 24 hours. I got my check, the gate was opened up, and I was a free man.

15

THE TRANSITION

When I walked outside the gate and into the parking lot I saw my sister Yakini and Theresa waiting for me. I was so happy to be free and from the looks on their faces, they were just as happy as I was. I gave them both a hug and we hopped in Yakini's car. After they asked me why it took so long for me to come out and how it felt to be free, I told them to take me to the closest fast food restaurant.

We drove to a Burgerville restaurant in Vancouver and I felt like I was in Heaven. The last time I had been outside of the gates of Larch it was to go to a dentist appointment. Although I wasn't cuffed and got to go to a regular dentist office, I knew that right when I was done I would be returning to prison. This time, I was bout to be hopping on I-5 north and heading back to Tacoma to start my life over. I was really free! I ordered three regular cheeseburgers, a large fry and a milkshake and I swear it was the best food I had ever eaten in my life.

When we got back to Tacoma I had my sister take me straight to check in with the probation officer. I learned that I did not have set days when I had to report. They just had to complicate things. I was going to have to call a phone number every single day to find out if I had to come in or not. I also was going to have to complete three months of outpatient drug treatment. Besides that, all I had to do was stay out of trouble and deal with random visits at home.

I had always been told that probation is extremely hard and that it makes life pretty much impossible. Fortunately for me, the people who told me that only had bad experiences because they made bad choices and violated their probation. Some of the people who warned me believed that accepting the drug offender sentencing alternative was a set up because a lot of people have their DOSA revoked and end up serving all of their time. I had my mind made up that I was going to live my life right so I wasn't very concerned.

My next stop was to go see my kids. At the time of my release Nariya was four years old and Amare was just about to turn three. I was very happy to get to hold them and hug them. They also seemed happy to be able to see me without having to drive a long distance to the prison. I'm glad that they were so young while I was incarcerated because they didn't really understand what was going on. I'm sure they missed having my presence around but at their age they couldn't possibly understand the gravity of one of their parents being in prison.

After grabbing the kids, we went to my mom's apartment in Lakewood where I got to see her and my other sisters. I also got to see my step-dad, Fred, for the first time since being in the county. He didn't come to visit while I was in prison. I also got to meet my niece and nephew for the first time. I never made it to see Nikki's son because I got locked up the day after he was born and Yakini had her daughter while I was in the county jail.

After catching up with my closest family members I met up with my homeboy Mo and my cousin Jay. Mo gave me a bunch of clothes and some shoes. I was extremely grateful because I had nothing. Everything I owned before turning myself in was gone. He also gave me some money. Jay and Yakini gave me money as well. I appreciated having people look out for me. I was really feeling the love.

I also had a couple other people look out for me. My homeboy Jason, who I mentioned wrote me while I was in prison, invited me to come to a high-school basketball game at Lincoln and he paid for me to get in with a $100 bill and allowed me to keep the change. My sister Sareeta's ex-boyfriend, Wayne, also looked out for me by fixing a car for me and instead of allowing me to pay him he gave me a $100 bill when he was done. I really appreciate people like that.

Although I was already released, Theresa was still going through the court process and we didn't know what would happen with her case. Yes, in the time that I hired a lawyer, turned myself in, went through the court process, served all my time, and was released, she was still going to court. She was my co-defendant but here I was a free man and she could be on her way to prison. There was no way she was going to have to do as much time as me because she is a female, so I was hoping for the best.

In order to satisfy my probation officer and start making a little bit of money, I got a job at the Old Country Buffet. We also had signed up for benefits through DSHS. I was able to get food stamps, cash, clothing vouchers, hygiene vouchers, and more through DSHS and that helped a lot. Theresa had a job at a store in the mall called Papaya but shortly after I got out of prison she walked out during one of her shifts and never went back. My job at the Old Country Buffet only lasted a couple shifts before I realized that I wasn't going to be able to make it there and quit.

We were pretty much back at square one. Neither one of us had a real income. We were highly dependent on welfare. I tried telling myself that we could only go up from there, that things could only get better. I decided I wasn't going to wait around to see what happened with Theresa's case before taking steps to make things better. I decided that I was going to enroll in school at Pierce College to try to make something of myself. If I wanted to be able to open doors to support my family without taking penitentiary chances, I knew that education would be the key.

A couple major things happened in between me being released from prison and starting college. In August we found out that Theresa was pregnant with our second child together and our third overall. Despite the fact that I was broke, I was going to have to tough it out until an opportunity arose because I refused to go back to prison. The kid that Theresa was pregnant with was never going to have to experience being away from their father. There would be no jailhouse or prison visits. I was going to go earn a college degree and be successful so that I could take care of my family.

Unfortunately, right as I was beginning my journey as a college student, Theresa's case had come to an end. She accepted a plea deal and was going to be sentenced to one year and one day in prison. She had all but three or four of her charges dropped. With good time, she would have to serve a total of six months. She was going to have to serve this prison time while pregnant. When we walked into the courtroom on her plea date we were hoping that she would come back later to be sentenced, just as I was, but that didn't happen. They took her away immediately. It's funny how the person who was out on bail was sentenced immediately while the person who was in custody had to wait several weeks.

Once Theresa was locked up, I no longer felt comfortable living at her mom's house. I had been out of prison for several months by then and it was time for me to move forward and get a place. However, there was no clear path to finding a place of my own. I didn't know what I was going to do but I knew that returning to a life of crime was not the answer.

Due to the fact that I was receiving cash assistance from the state, I was required to participate in the WorkFirst program. This came along with a requirement that I spend at least 30 hours per week doing approved activities. Those activities can include working, school, community service, and job search, amongst other things. Nariya was just starting Kindergarten but the kids were enrolled at a daycare that picked her up after school so luckily I didn't have any barriers to doing what I needed to do. I went from being an inmate with very little responsibility to now being the person responsible for two small children and this was a major motivating force in me wanting to live my life the right way.

I ended up meeting the WorkFirst requirements by participating in a job search program, doing "volunteer" work, and by being enrolled in school. Initially, it was a battle to have being in school count as an approved activity because the people who made the rules decided that WorkFirst participants should only pursue academic programs that were one year or less and led to a certificate rather than a degree. I saw this as being very restricting and enforcing the oppression of poor people. A lot of people rely on state benefits and pursuing a college degree is one of the best ways to climb out of those circumstances. Although it will take longer, anyone who wants to earn a degree should be allowed to without someone discouraging, or especially, forbidding it.

I spent time "volunteering" at the Tacoma Rescue Mission and St. Vincent De Paul thrift store. At the Rescue Mission, I had to help prepare and serve meals to homeless people. I found this to be very rewarding. Everyone who I served a meal to seemed to be very grateful. It made me feel good to participate in providing meals to people who otherwise might not have been able to eat. At St. Vincent De Paul, I helped collect donated items from people. I also spent time doing random tasks such as cleaning, helping load or unload things, and even assisting customers.

I am a strong believer in the idea that when people do good they get good in return. I feel like ever since I turned my life around I have received blessing, after blessing, after blessing. After Theresa got taken off to prison I felt trapped but I wanted to move out of her mom's house as soon as possible. Her mom never made me feel uncomfortable or unwelcomed but I had pride issues as well as a desire to be more independent and able to move freely without worrying about when I would finally wear out my welcome. Fortunately for me, there was a major blessing about to come my way.

One day I was on Pacific avenue in Tacoma participating in WorkFirst job search activities. On my way out, once I was done, I noticed that there was a housing agency sharing the same building I was in. I walked in and there was a man standing there. I asked him if he knew of any housing agencies that worked with people with a criminal history.

I also told him that I had two young children as well. The man responded by saying, "Today is your lucky day, I am in a good mood." He then placed a call and told the person on the other end of the phone that he had someone who needed a two-bedroom, who also had a criminal history, and he wanted them to do all they could to take care of me. After a short conversation he hung up the phone, wrote down a name and address, and told me to go there on Monday. This happened on a Friday so it was the very next business day.

The place that he sent me to is called the Lakewood Area Shelter Association (LASA). They are an organization that offers many services to people who are living in poverty, with housing being one of them. He sent me to speak with a woman named Paula who was one of the people in charge at LASA.

When I arrived at LASA I asked for Paula and she brought me back to her office. She told me about their housing program which provides much more to families than just a place to stay. Residents of their housing program have their lives enriched by participating in monthly gatherings that feature speakers who have information or resources to share in the areas of education, banking, home ownership, employment, mental health, and many other areas. They also help families with various needs such as clothing, furniture, toys, books, gas vouchers and more. Paula informed me that they had a long waiting list to get into this program, however, due to the fact that the person who called is who he is, she was going to give me a unit that had just opened up and it would be ready for us to move in by Wednesday. Rent would be 30% of my income and my criminal history was of no concern to her so there were no barriers.

I felt so blessed in that moment. If I had walked into that housing agency at another time, I might have spoken with someone else. I happened to be in the right place at the right time and I feel like it was no coincidence, but rather, by design. I was provided with exactly what I needed, exactly when I needed it. God is good.

By Wednesday I had the keys and it was a reality, only months removed from my release from prison, I had my own place. We were placed in a duplex in the Parkland area that had a nice big yard. It was small, but perfect for us. LASA made sure that we had everything we needed when we moved in. I will forever be grateful for their generosity. If I ever get rich, they will have a huge donation coming their way from me. They did so much for us. They made sure my kids had a great Christmas and everything. I appreciate them so much.

In addition to LASA, I had support coming from Theresa's mom still as well. There was a time when my car had broken down and she made a $1,000 down payment for me to get a new one. She also helped a lot with the kids. I was very happy to have her.

I had enrolled Nariya in school at Spanaway Elementary. Although I wasn't her biological father, her mom had signed over power of attorney to me and I was able to take care of everything I needed to take care of. I was happy that I got to keep Nariya and Amare together. I was worried that Nariya's dad or another blood relative might have tried to step in and take care of her while Theresa served her prison time but we never ran into any issues of that sort. Nariya continued to visit with her dad and he was fully cooperative and cool with her living with me.

It wasn't long before we had gotten used to our daily routine. Every day I would take Nariya and Amare to daycare bright and early in the morning. They were going to a home-based daycare and it was very convenient because the lady would drive Nariya to school and pick her up every day. I usually had a class that would start at 8 a.m. at Pierce College. I was taking three classes at the time, a total of 12 credits. After going to class I would have to immediately leave campus and either go do my job search activities or my "volunteer" work per WorkFirst conditions. I would normally be rushing afterward to pick up the kids by 6 when the daycare was essentially closed although it was at someone's house.

This period of my life was a very difficult period but I felt like I managed it well. I was dealing with a lot of issues that could have led me down a path of destruction. Instead, I used my circumstances as motivation to keep moving forward and making progress so that my kids would never have to go through the types of things I went through as a kid. I was months removed from my release from prison, my kid's mom had just been sent to prison, I was on probation, I was receiving welfare and had to meet WorkFirst requirements, plus I was in my first quarter as a college student. I had a lot on my plate.

If this was a test, I'd say I passed with flying colors. I didn't have the best grades that first quarter of college but I made it. I was taking Math 54, which is pre-algebra, middle school math. Despite having a horrible history with math, I was able to pass this class with a 2.5. I also took a class called "Choosing a Major", which was designed to help people like me decide on an academic path moving forward. When I first enrolled in school I didn't know exactly what I wanted to pursue. These types of classes never go well for me, I passed with a 2.2 but I didn't like this class.

The one class that I did well in was the one real college class I took, that was English Composition 1, or English 101. I did extremely well in this class and received nothing but great feedback on my papers. I earned a 3.8 in this class. The fact that I didn't do so well in math but did great in writing is simply the story of my life. Either way, I finished my first quarter with a 2.99 gpa and this gave me confidence that I could succeed going forward. These were the first classes that I had passed since the 8th grade so I really needed the confidence boost.

My kids were happy and healthy despite the unfortunate circumstance of having one parent come home from prison just for the other to leave for prison. We had a roof over our head, we had transportation. I was handling business. Plus, Theresa wasn't serving a long sentence so she would be home soon. I hadn't been out of prison for half of a year yet, but I felt like I was in a great place.

16
PROGRESS

By the time 2009 rolled around I was about to start my second quarter of college. I was basically a single parent at the time raising two small children but things were going well. I was doing just fine with my probation and I was in compliance with any requirements DSHS had for me.

My family was doing ok at this time, based on the standards that had been set throughout my life, but not as great as they could have or should have been. My mom and Fred were up to their usual thing, getting high, letting people live with them. This was what's normal for them. A lot of my aunts and uncles who smoked crack had stopped and did better for themselves, but these guys just couldn't quit permanently. In addition to being stuck in their addiction, along with Nikki, they were constantly in and out of the hospital as well. It always seemed like if there wasn't one thing wrong, it was another.

Sareeta was battling several issues as well. While I was in prison her kids went to live with their dads. Her kid's dads both ended up in prison. When her sons' dad went to prison he left the kids with his family members and his family members ran off and kept them from my sister. Despite her life circumstances, she has rights as a parent, and her kids should have never been taken away by people who had no rights to them. I don't see how it can be considered anything besides kidnapping but my sister was offered no help by authorities in locating her children. They remained out of her life for years.

My cousins who I was closest to growing up were still out looking for the next lick or come up. They weren't making bank lick type money but they also weren't trying to go get a job. It's not easy to leave the paper chase behind when it's been such a big part of your life for so long. There wasn't anyone knocking on their door or calling their phones offering opportunities either.

It's easy to look at my family and judge them based off what they choose to do or not do with their life. However, while people love to point the finger at rotten apples, they don't seem to like pointing their finger at the trees that keep producing these rotten apples. No one wants to look at the systems in place that go back generations that led to the mindset, values, and behaviors that my family had. Our grandparents were impacted by racism and discrimination, our parents were destroyed by drug abuse that could largely be blamed on racism and discrimination, and we are the victims of poor parenting and poor environments that are exacerbated by racism and discrimination.

I do not mean to imply that because we are a black family, we can't do good. However, when you are a disadvantaged minority, and you face our circumstances, it is often hard to find the support and resources to climb out of those circumstances. My mom had the desire to quit using drugs, she went to treatment. However, when reality hit her in the face and she was stuck living in shelters and poor drug-filled neighborhoods, it would take a level of strength she did not have to avoid the pitfalls.

As for me, no matter what, I was going to follow the path I was on all the way to success. I wanted to be different. I wanted to be the one who had that strength to stay the course and not be influenced to throw my life away. I was going to be the one who decided that we were not innocent kids anymore and as adults we had to make the decision to be positive and productive members of society despite our circumstances. Once you are grown, you know right from wrong. You might not know the steps you need to take to turn your life around but you know when you are not living right. I decided that integrity was important to me and I was going to live my life in a way that could only lead to positive outcomes. I was no longer going to participate in any criminal activity and no amount of money would entice me to change my mind.

In Winter quarter I went from having one class in which I had over a 3.0 to having two. Despite this improvement, my GPA dipped due to a 1.7 grade in a class I didn't like very much. I came to realize that I needed to make sure that I was always in classes that interested me because I would not work hard if I didn't care about what I was learning. I had two early examples of that in the choosing a major class and now in a computer information systems class.

My routine was pretty much the same this quarter as it was the last. At the end of the quarter, it was time for Theresa to come home. She was released on my birthday, March 23rd, 2009. She was almost nine months pregnant when she was released. It's as if everything was planned out perfectly for us by a higher power. Somehow it worked out where she was with the kids while I was in prison, I was with the kids while she was in prison, and she was due to give birth immediately following her release. Although it wasn't intentional, the timing worked out perfectly.

When Theresa got released she got out to a much more comfortable situation than I did. She didn't have to worry about the future in regards to our court proceedings and we had our own place. She also didn't have to serve any time on probation so there was nothing hanging over her head. Theresa gave birth to my second son, Frelimo Omari Amili Jr., on April 11th, 2009. Our full family was together and we didn't have to look over our shoulder or worry about anyone being sent away. We could actually move forward as we had previously tried to do when we moved to Portland but this time we weren't hindered by the thought of being pulled back by the criminal justice system.

I decided around this time that I was going to get my associate's degree in Human Services Substance Abuse. I had a couple solid quarters under my belt as a college student and I felt like I would do well. Theresa being home also made life a lot easier. We were able to take the kids out of daycare because she could stay home with them. Nariya started to take a school bus to school and life became a lot easier. I spent the rest of 2009 getting more alcoholism & drug abuse classes under my belt and progressing toward earning my degree. I also continued progressing through the math classes that I had to pass before finally getting to the college level. I had to take three non-college level classes total before finally being able to take college level statistics. I spent a lot of time learning the math that I should have learned as a child while I was at Pierce College.

Theresa didn't work for the first year following her release from prison. Fortunately, when you give birth, you are exempt from having to participate in WorkFirst. We lived off of cash benefits, food stamps, WIC, and financial aid. While we weren't financially stable as we desired to be, things were going good for us.

After I had some of the chemical dependency classes under my belt I decided that I would apply for work study so that I could bring in some extra money. One of the work study positions that was open was at a counseling agency so I figured that would be a good opportunity for me to get some work experience and also get my foot in the door in the field I planned to enter. I applied, went in for an interview, and got the job.

I was surprised to see that the entire counseling agency was ran by a black family. The business was ran by a mother, father and son. They all seemed like cool people and I was happy to be provided the opportunity to work with them. They wanted me to jump right in and work with a caseload providing treatment services as a CDPT, which is a checmical dependency professional trainee. Many of my classmates were employed as CDPTs and managed their own caseloads but I had heard a lot of horror stories. A lot of agencies seem to be willing to put their clients at risk by having someone who is inexperienced and in over their head be their primary treatment provider. I avoided this because I was scared of rejection and I didn't believe that my application to be a licensed CDPT would be approved due to the fact that I was currently on probation. I never submitted my application and I didn't feel quite ready for that anyway. I ended up basically filing papers and creating documents for a couple months before running into issues with being paid and being forced to resign.

By this time it was early 2010 and Theresa's exemption from WorkFirst activities was coming to an end. She applied for a job at Jack in The Box near our house and we immediately got off of cash benefits. Getting off cash benefits was like a breath of fresh air. While we still received food stamps, there is no WorkFirst required for that. The humiliating days of having to approach my teachers, in front of my classmates, asking them to sign a paper verifying I was actually in class were over. I felt like I was set free.

It was around this time when I began to take out student loans as well. Initially, I relied exclusively on grants in order to pay for school and school-related expenses. Eventually, I decided that it might be worth taking on some debt in order to avoid having to work while I was in school. I didn't want to have to worry about being able to pay for things but I also didn't want to have to sacrifice being successful in school in order to bring money in. Loans seemed like the obvious solution.

Theresa began to work the graveyard shift and life became very stable and smooth for us. We had it set up to where when I was at school, she was at home, and when she was at work, I was at home. However, the housing program that we were in was only two years long and by October of 2010 we were going to have to move. We began to worry a little bit about what would happen by the time October rolled around because we could not afford to pay full rent. We also both had recent felony convictions on our record and although LASA didn't hold that against us, they probably would have if not for one phone call.

By the Summer of 2010, we had gotten great news. Well, the first great news we had gotten was that Theresa was pregnant with our third son and our fourth child overall. Additionally, we found out that Theresa's name had finally reached the top of Pierce County Housing's waiting list after a five-year wait. While we were happy that there was potentially a way out of us being forced to either be homeless or move back in with Theresa's mom, we didn't know how they might react to our criminal histories.

Although Theresa had come up on the waiting list for housing we still had to go through an application process. This process included background checks. When we received the decision from Pierce County Housing we were devastated to find out that we were denied based on our criminal history. These sorts of denials have the potential to send people who are trying to turn their lives around right back into a life of crime. Housing is one of life's key necessities and even people who have been in trouble with the law deserve to have a roof over their head. We had young children and another baby on the way but that didn't matter because the piece of paper that printed out of their machine showed convictions in our past.

I decided that I was not going to stand for this. It was now 2010 and I had not hit a bank lick since 2005. Although I spent time in prison, I was now doing something positive with my life. I felt like I was on a mission to help people and that people like me should be given every opportunity to make something of themselves. If an agency's mission is to help the disadvantaged then how could they possibly justify denying help to people who are amongst the most disadvantaged? We are not only disadvantaged from being poor but we are also being ostracized to the extent that a government agency doesn't deem us worthy of having a roof over our head. If they won't rent to us, then who will?

One thing that a lot of people don't notice is that most denial letters come with instructions on how to appeal decisions. I wrote a very long letter explaining the progress that I had made in my life up to this point and the fact that I should not be judged based on my actions from before I was old enough to purchase liquor. Theresa was working, I was a college student, people like us should be supported rather than ostracized. We are exactly who you should be aiming to support. Luckily, the people who make decisions regarding appeals agreed with the points that I made in the letter. We were required to take a class called Ready to Rent and by August we were moving in to a four-bedroom house, with a garage, and a nice big yard. Like LASA, they would charge us 30% of our income for rent.

Once again, we were blessed, and right on time. I began to believe that as long as I remained positive and kept doing good, I would continue to be blessed. I had no desire to return to any type of criminal activity. I was not going to allow myself to fail. I was going to earn my degree no matter what. We had a place to call home that didn't come along with any time limits, our family was growing, Theresa was working, and I was using education as a tool to transform my failures into success.

The nature of the classes that I was taking had a great impact on my life. It's hard to constantly read about, write about, and discuss problems regarding criminality, addiction, negative social circles and disadvantaged backgrounds without applying what I have learned to my own life. There were also a lot of parallels with what I learned in these classes and what I learned while participating in the drug treatment and behavior modification that came along with my DOSA sentence. I was acquiring all of the information I needed in order to avoid going back to my previous lifestyle. The changes in my values, beliefs, and behaviors that resulted from acquiring this information was inevitable.

My third son was born on December 10th, 2010. We felt like with the birth of Amaru, our family was complete. In the 2.5 years since my release we went from a small family of four to what could be considered a large family of six. I knew at that point that if I was going to be able to give my family a good life in the future, I was going to have to continue to sacrifice and go hard in the pursuit of my education. I didn't see any other path that could lead me to a place where I would be able to make an honest living without being stuck in poverty. There wasn't a lot of money to be made being a chemical dependency professional but pursing a degree in this field could be a stepping stone to a career and success in the future.

As I continued progressing toward earning my degree I started having second thoughts about wanting to be a drug and alcohol counselor. A lot of the stories that my classmates told after being active in the field really turned me off. There seemed to be a lot of people who were over worked and not really seeing the impact being made that they intended. The field in general seemed to have a lot of issues. One of the biggest issues was the battle between mental health professionals and chemical dependency professionals in regards to the treatment of people with co-occurring disorders. I have learned that anyone treating people with co-occurring mental health and substance abuse disorders should be trained in both and they definitely shouldn't be treated by someone who just began school to become a drug and alcohol counselor a matter of months ago. In addition to that, many of the people who my classmates were treating were court ordered and I want to work with people who decided on their own to take steps to better their life. People who are court-ordered might really want to change but their motivations for being in treatment and their outcomes are different than the person who made the decision on their own.

Eventually I learned that it would be possible to transfer to the University of Washington's Tacoma campus on a direct transfer agreement if I earned my degree and had at least a 2.75 gpa. I knew that the gpa requirement would not be an issue so I decided that this would be my end goal for my time at Pierce, as opposed to beginning a career in the chemical dependency field.

I was really inspired by a classmate of mine at Pierce who had already graduated from there but came back to add chemical dependency credentials to the mental health credentials that he already had. This guy had served time in prison for a drive-by shooting and when he got out he went straight to college just like I had done. Once he finished at Pierce he went on to the University of Washington where he earned his Bachelor's and Master's degrees. I was amazed by his story and the fact that someone could get out of prison and actually become a student at UW. I was also a Husky fan and going to UW always seemed like some unreachable dream for me. Little did I know, I had a direct path.

With my new goal not far from reach, I continued to push forward with my education. Before I knew it, Spring quarter of 2011 had rolled around and I was at the doorstep of graduation. I had already gone through the process of applying for admission at UW Tacoma. When my acceptance letter came, it brought me to a level of joy that I can't quite describe. I was the same guy who first dropped out in the 6th grade. I struggled so much when it came to school as a kid and ultimately I fell victim to the school-to-prison pipeline after failing to graduate from high school. But here I was, on the verge of earning a college degree and transferring to the University of Washington to be a Husky. Unfortunately, a month before graduation, my whole world got shaken up.

I had mentioned previously that my mom and Fred were constantly in and out of the hospital. The same is true for my sister, Nikki. They all suffered from diabetes and congestive heart failure. Of the three, Nikki seemed to have it the worst because her diabetes had gone unmanaged since childhood.

Toward the beginning of 2011 Fred was hospitalized. Whenever he would go to the hospital he would tell the doctors that he was complying with everything he was supposed to do as far as his eating habits, refraining from smoking and drug use, and taking his medicine. After this visit, doctors apparently decided to throw in the towel on treating Fred. They determined that he was not getting any better and that they had no other options but to put him in hospice care. Hospice care means they take away all medications and treatments that are keeping you alive and simply provide comfort meds until you die. This was devastating news for our whole family. It seemed like Fred didn't want to accept what he was told.

Keep in mind that this man has spent far more time being in the lives of me and my sisters than our own dads have. He obviously wasn't in competition with our dads but he was the more present father figure, for better or for worse. To be told that he was dying was the worst and most heartbreaking thing that I ever had to hear in my life. I did not want it to be true.

Over the months leading into May, he went from standing and talking and seeming close to his usual self, to completely deteriorating and sleeping more than anything. He was not supposed to eat a lot of salt or anything like that but it was hard for me to tell him no when I would ask if he wanted anything and his request was something from McDonald's. How do you refuse someone who is dying regardless something that might bring them a little joy? Could it get him closer to death? Possibly, but I just wanted him to go out on his own terms. He was adamant about wanting to be at home rather than in a nursing home or hospice house and it was clear that he had come to grips with his fate and just wanted to live his last days as close to normal as possible.

On Friday, May 13th, 2011, I stopped by my Mom and Fred's house. I had to drive down their street every single day on my way to school so it was always convenient to stop by. Fred was sleeping in bed but when he would breath there was a gurgling sound. There was clearly fluid somewhere it shouldn't be. I stood in the room watching him, knowing that he could be gone at any time. I left to go to class and told my mom I'd be back later.

When I stopped by on my way back home I walked in to find my mom crying frantically. Fred had taken his final breath moments before I arrived. I went into the bedroom and grabbed his cold hand. I couldn't believe I was looking at the lifeless body of someone so close to me. It was hard for me to accept the fact that I would never be able to speak to my step-dad again. I would never get to hear him talk shit. He could never make me laugh again.

Fred's body stayed in that room all day as people came to say their goodbyes and pay their respects. He had three biological children, one had been violently murdered in the years prior to Fred's death but the other two, Cubby and Rashonda, immediately came up to Tacoma from Portland to say goodbye to their father. It wasn't until the late hours of the night when his body was finally picked up and taken away.

After Fred passed away we had to try to gather up some money and arrange for a funeral and cremation. Fred had always spoken of having a burial plot next to his mother and father but we could not afford to bury him there. When you get together a bunch of people who have no money and they put all of their money together, there is still no money. After having several discussions with high-priced funeral homes that were out of our financial reach, we had to settle for the smallest, cheapest, most ghetto funeral home imaginable. We were only able to "settle" for this place, because they allowed us to finance most of the cost.

When it came time to go to Fred's viewing before the funeral we were hit with the harsh reality that you get what you pay for. Fred looked nothing like himself and there was a strong odor coming from his body as if he hadn't been embalmed. It was obvious that the funeral home was trying to take as many shortcuts as possible. We didn't have a lot of people chipping in or making contributions so we had to do what we had to do.

The funeral was the most emotional moment of my life up to that point. His death was the first death that I ever actually had to deal with. When my mom's parents died I was just a kid. Although I was present when my grandma had the heart attack that killed her I didn't really understand what was going on and I didn't have to play a role in planning her funeral. None of my mom or dad's siblings had passed away at this point, I never had any close cousins or relatives die. I had never even been to a funeral, if I did go to my grandparents' funerals I don't remember it.

My mom was now without her life partner. Although their relationship was never perfect they had been together a very long time. I didn't know how my mom would respond to losing her husband. I was very worried for her. Even worse, she had the same exact health problems that he had. To be honest, it had always seemed like both her and Nikki were in worse health than Fred. I was very scared for my mom. I didn't want to lose her. As hard as it was to cope with losing my step-dad, it would have to be a million times worse if I were to lose my mom. I also didn't want her to be unhappy and miserable and lose her desire to live. I felt powerless to do anything to make things better for her.

17
THE HUSKY

When Fred died I was approaching the end of my time at Pierce College. I was in the final month of my last quarter before earning my degree. While dealing with the loss and having to plan a funeral that no one in my family could afford impacted me, I did not allow it to stop me from doing what I needed to do. I refused to dishonor Fred by failing in his name. I wasn't going to be one of those people who uses tragic life events as an excuse to halt all progress and become stagnant.

In order to earn my degree, I was forced to make sacrifices in terms of my workload in school. I decided that I was going to completely ignore one of my three classes for the rest of the quarter. I didn't need the credits for that class in order to graduate. I knew that the best thing for me to do would be to limit my responsibilities and focus only on the most important classes that I actually needed. I was enrolled in Spanish 2, Business Writing, and Speed Reading and Speed Reading was the class I chose to sacrifice.

Although it was difficult, I managed to earn the final credits that I needed in order to earn my degree and transfer to the University of Washington's Tacoma campus. I finished the quarter with a 2.42 gpa which was my lowest grade point average out of any of the quarters I attended Pierce College. I really struggled to make it through the Spanish class but I did pretty well in Business Writing. It's no coincidence that my worst quarter was the quarter in which tragedy struck my family.

In June of 2011, I graduated with an Associate of Arts degree as well as a certificate in Alcoholism & Drug Abuse. I participated in the commencement ceremony at the Tacoma Dome and my mom and dad were both present amongst many other loved ones to watch me walk across that stage. This was a great moment for me because I felt like it made up for the fact that I never graduated from high school. Despite my horrible academic background I was actually a college graduate. Despite the fact that I was a dropout and a convicted felon who had served time in prison, here I was doing something positive that took time, commitment, and hard work. I made my parents proud.

My mom always bragged about me to everyone. Every time she introduced me to one of her friends she would tell them I am a counselor. I made sure to correct her every time and let her know that although I was in school to be a counselor, I was not actually a counselor. She didn't care, she was so proud of the fact that I was doing something positive with my life.

In the Summer of 2011, following my graduation, I had my first break from being a student in two and a half years. While I was working on earning my degree at Pierce I didn't take the Summers off. I was a full-time student year-round. However, after I graduated, I used the Summer of 2011 to relax, have fun, and further cope with the recent loss of my step-dad.

My three years of probation were up that June and I felt like I was actually free for the first time in a long time. Community custody obviously gives you a lot more freedom than being in jail or prison but you still don't feel free. You can be sent to jail or prison without even committing a new crime. You have to call every single day to see if you have to report and if you forget to call you have to nervously wait and hope you didn't miss your day. You have to deal with random visits to your house by your probation officer who normally brings a friend with him to walk through your living room, bedrooms, and hallways.

Although I was happy to be off probation, I knew that being on probation was one of the contributing factors to me turning my life around. That constant threat of incarceration, even for things that weren't an actual crime, helped motivate me to do the right thing. I feel like if I was released from prison and didn't have probation, like Theresa, I might have been more willing to entertain risky behaviors and situations. I would be lying if I said that fear of consequences didn't influence my decision making following my release from prison.

The Summer seemed to fly by and before I knew it, it was time for new student orientation at the University of Washington. When I showed up I had thoughts running through my head that I might not belong. Had they made some sort of mistake? The materials being handed out have the same W logo and the purple and gold that I grew up admiring. This is the same school that Nate Robinson, Brandon Roy, and Corey Dillon went to, just a different campus. I was actually a Washington Husky. I obviously wasn't a student athlete, like I had dreamed about as a kid, but I was a college student at the University of Washington three years after being released from prison.

In my family, there are not many people who I would say are successful. Due to this, the simple fact that I was starting school at UW made me a success story in the eyes of many of my family members. Simply being a college student earned me the praise that you would expect from someone who had already graduated with several degrees and made it to the top of their professional field. I had the full support of my loved ones and I wanted to make sure to succeed so that I didn't let them down. I was under a lot of pressure but I embraced it. I wanted to show my cousins and anyone else who grew up the way I did that we actually had options. If I failed, then it would be hard to deliver that message. Success was my only option.

My first quarter at UW was a mix of good and bad. At new student orientation, we were required to pick our class schedule for our first quarter. New students at orientation basically get the leftovers after continuing students get to register. A lot of classes were already full at this point. Additionally, many of us had no idea what classes we actually needed to take. Surprisingly, we were advised to pretty much get into any class we could that sounded interesting to us and had space.

As part of my financial aid package I was awarded work study and I decided that I should take advantage of that as an opportunity to gain work experience and to become more of a part of the campus community. I felt like I could have developed a lot more had I been more involved at Pierce rather than simply showing up to class and leaving. That was in large part due to life circumstances but I wanted to change it.

I turned in a resume for a position as a student assistant in the Advancement Office at UWT. My resume was horrible, and nearly blank outside of earning my Associate's degree, but I was asked to come in for an interview anyway. That is one of the great things about student jobs, they know you are a work in progress and under development. There was no job application and no background checks. I was a member of the Husky family and that appeared to be all that mattered in terms of being eligible to work on campus.

When I showed up to the interview I was surprised to be greeted by a panel of three people. The panel members took turns asking me questions and I got the sense that the interview was going very well. They asked me a wide variety of questions about how I might handle situations that could arise and I did my best to answer truthfully while also making a good impression. They were highly interested in how I might cope with stressful situations and I told them that I am a "weirdo" and I don't feel stress. My whole life I have been forced to rely on resiliency to cope with situations that could be considered stressors and I have the ability to stay positive and focused in the face of adversity.

At the end of the interview they told me they had a couple other candidates and that they would inform me of their decision later on that week. The very next day I got a call and they not only offered me the position I had interviewed for, but I was also offered an additional Media Tech position that paid more per hour but wasn't as consistent in terms of hours. Normally, a student wouldn't hold more than one position on campus but since the Media Tech job was scheduled only as needed, I was able to.

For my first quarter, I ended up registering for a literature class that focused on women's literature, a communications class focused on writing mass media, and an interdisciplinary studies seminar. I did very well in the literature class, earning a 3.4, and in the seminar, earning a 4.0. However, I earned a 0.0 in the communications class.

The communications class that I was in was for communications majors who were studying to enter the field of journalism. The class was all about writing and formatting news stories and articles. The professor was really tough, as she was training students to become professionals who were great at their craft. Although I was completely out of place, I did very well for over half of the quarter.

Things went bad for me when we were required to set up interviews with individuals in the professional world, outside of class time, in order to write our stories. Me and Theresa were still alternating, where she was home with the kids while I was on campus, and I was home with the kids while she was at work. I really didn't have a lot of opportunity outside of class and work to meet and interview someone, and I also was intimidated by the task. I still felt like I might not belong at this prestigious university. Would anyone really be willing to meet with a convicted felon for an interview? Should I even tell them I am a convicted felon? If I don't, am I doing something wrong? I felt like the task was too much for me at the time so I stopped attending the class. I completed everything up to that point satisfactorily but I decided that I couldn't complete the final paper which required me to interview people.

Despite failing one of my first three classes, I felt good about my first quarter as a Husky. It would have been easy to look at that 0.0 grade and have it further enhance my reservations about whether or not I belonged, but instead I decided to focus on the fact that I already had a 4.0 under my belt and that I had earned a 3.4 in a class I probably had no business in.

Around Christmas, my mom told me and my sisters that she decided she was going to move to California. I was concerned because we had always had each other around. Even while I was locked up my mom came to visit so there has never been a period when my mom wasn't a part of my life. I knew she would be only a phone call away but that wasn't the same as having her here and being able to go visit and eat her great cooking. Besides, something just didn't quite seem right. My mom had just recently lost her husband, did she really want to lose her kids too?

I tried to tell her not to go but there was no stopping her. She had her mind made up. We spent Christmas together at Theresa's mom's house, my dad was there, everyone was there. Me, Yakini and Sareeta didn't know when or how we would see our mom again so it was a scary and emotional time for us. She also was still having health problems. She was in and out of the hospital still. It wasn't long before she decided to move that I sat with her in the emergency room and listened to doctors tell her that the medicine she needed would not be covered by her insurance. They even asked her "what would you do if you had to either have this medicine or die" and her answer was that she would obviously just have to die. She could not afford to pay for the meds. I didn't feel comfortable at all with her moving to California but I had no say in it.

So, I mentioned that in my first quarter I took classes in three different disciplines. In my second quarter, I did the same thing again, however, it was three completely different ones. In Winter, 2012, I registered in a criminal justice class titled Police and Society, an education class titled School and Society, and a history class titled History of Christianity. I didn't enroll in these classes for any reason besides the fact that they sounded interesting to me. I had no real focus.

I had declared as a major in the Interdisciplinary Arts & Sciences program under the Self & Society concentration. Fortunately for me, although I was taking random classes, they all seemed to meet some sort of requirement for this degree program. This specific degree didn't have a set focus at all. None of the classes I was taking were related and there was no building upon prior knowledge. I didn't really notice this at the time, and as a first-generation college student, it didn't really make a difference to me. My goal was to earn a degree, I didn't have any specific career goals or anything.

Although the History of Christianity class was not interesting at all and I didn't do so well, I felt like I had improved in my second quarter. The Police & Society and School & Society classes were both highly interesting to me and I did do well in those classes.

I felt privileged to be who I am, coming from where I come from, and to still have the opportunity to take a class that was taught by a former FBI agent and full of people who want to go into criminal justice fields. I was one of very few students in the class who wasn't a criminal justice major and I am pretty sure I am the only one in the class who had served time in prison. We discussed topics such as police brutality, bias in policing, the role of police, laws, policies, and much more. It was nice to see that there are people who have worked in law enforcement who recognize that there are issues in terms of policing. Prior to entering this class, I had never had a positive experience with any type of law enforcement. Any interactions with them usually involved them trying to harass or arrest someone I cared about so it was very eye-opening to see that there are good cops out there who actually don't agree with or support bad cops.

In the School & Society class we read about and talked about so many important topics that played out in my own life. I was the only drop-out in the room, the only one in the room who hadn't learned much in the K-12 system, the only one who felt completely failed by the public-school system. I was able to speak from my experiences and enlighten those in the class who planned to go on to become educators. By sharing my perspective on the issues based on my experiences I provided value to my classmates.

At Pierce I had the opportunity to take some interesting and informative classes but my focus was mostly on alcoholism and drug abuse. At UWT, majoring in IAS: Self & Society, I had the opportunity to be exposed to so many more important subjects that I probably would not have been exposed to had I chose a different major.

It seems like in my life there are always good things happening and there are always bad things happening. It's almost as if there is an intentional balance between the good and the bad. During my second quarter at UWT it was no different.

Toward the beginning of the quarter I was with Theresa and my younger sister, Yakini, at Buffalo Wild Wings in Tacoma. The restaurant was fairly new and we wanted to try it out. When we got there, my sister noticed a large lump on my throat and asked me what it was. I didn't really know what she was talking about but I felt it and to my surprise there actually was a pretty large lump on my throat. I suffer from anxiety and seeing the worried look on my sister's face caused me to go into a panic attack. I began sweating profusely. I was extremely nervous and scared. I told my sister and Theresa that instead of eating we needed to go to the emergency room immediately. It was a cold night and I was so hot that right when I stepped outside of the building you could see steam leaving my body but no one else's.

When we arrived at the hospital I was so scared that I almost didn't want to find out what this lump was on my neck. I had already convinced myself that it was some form of cancer. Despite my fear, I went ahead and went through with finding out exactly what it was. I had to go through all kinds of tests and I was forced to do a CT scan. When I was going through the CT scan process I came to grips with the fact that I had cancer and I was going to die, probably immediately. Despite the fact that no one told me this and the testing was still in progress, I had made up my mind that this was the case. Once I returned from the scan and got back to the room they had me in I even told Theresa and Yakini that I had accepted the fact that I was dying and I wasn't in a position to complain or feel bad because so many little babies have died of cancer and they didn't get to see 27 years as I had. They both looked extremely scared for me but they tried to re-assure me that it didn't have to be cancer.

The wait to find out what was wrong seemed like it took forever. However, eventually I found out that I had a cyst on my neck that had probably been there since childhood but had recently gotten bigger. I was informed that most of the time, this type of cyst is not cancerous, however, I was going to have to undergo a major surgery to have it removed or else I could risk having problems in the future. Additionally, until I had the surgery I wouldn't know for sure if it was cancerous or benign. After being given this scary news, I was referred to an ear, nose, and throat specialist and sent on my way.

I was very worried. I had never had surgery before. What if it did end up being cancerous? What would that mean for me? What was it going to be like having my neck cut open? I didn't really want to find out, but I had to.

18

THE GOOD, THE BAD, THE UGLY

Before finding out that I would need surgery, Theresa, her mom, her sister and I had booked a trip to Orlando, Florida. Theresa's birthday is on February 23rd and we were all going to go to Disney World. I also wanted to go to some of the NBA All-Star weekend festivities which were taking place in Orlando that year. I had bought tickets for the NBA All-Star practice and the NBA Rookie vs Sophomore game. We also bought tickets to see Kevin Hart perform his "Laugh at my Pain" stand-up comedy show. Going to the All-Star game or the dunk contest would have been amazing but tickets to those events are so expensive that you only see rich people and celebrities there. That was something I considered to be out of reach.

I was very excited about this trip but I was concerned that the cyst on my neck would force me to miss it. Fortunately, when I met with the ear, nose and throat specialist who was going to perform my surgery, he informed me that there would be no risk involved with flying with the cyst. He also was willing to schedule the surgery during spring break so that I wouldn't have to miss any school. This was going to be a great vacation and I was very happy that my medical situation didn't ruin it for me.

When we booked this vacation I didn't realize it, but it was about to be a dream vacation for me. A couple days before leaving for Orlando, me and Theresa had to go to the welfare office to turn in some paperwork because we were receiving food stamps. During small talk with the DSHS employee who accepted our paperwork I had mentioned to her that we were going to Orlando that weekend. She responded by asking if we were going there for the NBA All-Star game. I told her that although we had tickets for a couple of the lower-priced all-star weekend events, we could never afford tickets to the actual all-star game. She informed me that she had a son who played in the NBA, and she would have him get tickets for us. She took down my name and cell phone number and told me that I would hear from her before I left for Orlando.

When she told me this, I didn't really have high expectations. My first reaction was skepticism. For one, I wondered why someone who played in the NBA's mother would be working at the welfare office. It wasn't high-paying work and surely her son would be taking care of her right? Additionally, I wondered if her son would actually have extra tickets to such a high-profile event lying around to give to a couple strangers.

To my surprise, she called me and told me that everything was good to go. Her son was going to provide us with tickets to not only the NBA All-Star game, but also to NBA All-Star Saturday Night which is when the dunk contest, three-point contest, and skills competition take place. She gave me the cell phone number of her son's agent and told me to call him when I got to Orlando so he could meet up with me to give me the tickets. I was so excited. I couldn't believe how lucky I was. What are the chances that we would be at the welfare office, meet an NBA player's mom, and be offered tickets to an event that I could have only dreamed of attending in person?

Right when we got off the plane in Orlando me, Theresa, and her sister Erin, had to immediately rush to the hotel. We didn't have much time to check in, get dressed, and leave for the Kevin Hart show. The show was at Universal Studios, which is also where the NBA on TNT had their *Inside the NBA* broadcast set up. While we were walking toward the show we got to see Shaq, Kenny, EJ and my old friend Charles Barkley doing their thing. The comedy show was so funny that I went to see it again when Kevin Hart's tour came to Seattle.

The next day we went to Disney World with Theresa's mom and sister before going our separate ways so that I could enjoy the All-Star weekend festivities. The Rookie vs Sophomore game was on Friday night, that was the first All-Star weekend event we went to. Theresa's birthday was a large part of the reason we were there but she knew how special this weekend was for me because I had always been a huge basketball fan. She didn't mind spending three straight days doing basketball related activities because there was time to do other things as well.

On Saturday, which was Theresa's birthday, we got right back to the basketball activities. First, we went to NBA All-Star Jam Session which is a family friendly event where fans get to meet players, get autographs and do a lot of other fun things. I got in contact with the agent of the player who was providing tickets for us and he met us right outside of Jam Session. Although the tickets were for upper-level seats, the face value was over $2,000. Once the tickets were in my hand it was finally real to me. We had really just been given a gift that will turn into a lifetime memory, and by a total stranger.

The woman who blessed me with this great gift's name is Alicia Winona Jones. Her son's name is Avery Bradley. He is from Tacoma, and plays in the NBA for the Boston Celtics. I will forever be grateful for these two, especially Alicia who did not have to go out of her way to make this happen. She unfortunately passed away in 2013 and I was devastated to hear the news. May her soul rest in peace. I had an amazing time on this vacation and she truly made it something I will never forget.

When I got back from Orlando it was toward the end of Winter quarter. I pretty much just had to finish the last few weeks of class and then it would be time to go under the knife. My mom had told me that she might be able to come back from California to support me during my surgery so although I was nervous, I was looking forward to my mom coming back in town.

Although I had taken a vacation in the middle of the quarter it didn't slow me down or impact me in a negative way. I finished the quarter with a 3.9 in School & Society, a 3.5 in Police & Society and a 1.7 in History of Christianity. I noticed that while the title of the history class sounded interesting to me, history, in general, was not my thing. History, as a discipline, is focused on dates and periods of time and that's something I mixed up a lot so that wasn't a good fit for me.

Some people might think it's weird for someone to average a 3.7 in two classes and then get a 1.7 in another, but for me, this was normal. I had a habit of doing the bare minimum to get by in classes that didn't have content that engaged with my interests or introduce me to something new and intriguing. If I wasn't getting deep into the classroom discussions, and if the material we read wasn't intriguing to me, I normally wouldn't do well in that class. The amount of time and effort that I put in has always been commensurate with my level of interest in the material. I knew that I didn't have to be a 4.0 student to succeed. I preferred to spend my time on the more interesting stuff, as opposed to spending a lot of time trying to master a topic that wasn't interesting to me, taking time away from those topics that are. You have to keep in mind that this was not me being a lazy student, it was me prioritizing. I had a lot of responsibilities, school was a part of my life but not my whole life.

Winter quarter ended on March 9th and I had surgery on March 20th. Unfortunately, my mom wasn't able to make it back because she wasn't feeling well. On the day of my surgery I was so scared. I couldn't stop thinking about all of the things that could possibly go wrong. Was I going to find out that I had cancer? Was I going to catch aids? Was I going to have a big scar on my neck? Was I going to wake up afterwards? Was I going to wake up in the middle of the procedure? My mind was all over the place and having anxiety definitely didn't help.

I remember getting to the hospital and having to go in by myself. Theresa dropped me off and she was going to pick me up when the surgery was over. The closer I got to the operating table, the more nervous I got.

As far as I know, I was passed out sleep during the surgery and didn't feel a thing. Once the drugs wore off and I woke up I noticed that I had a tube coming out of my throat. It was attached to a plastic bag where the drainage from the wound on my neck went. Come to find out, this tube was going to be stuck in my neck even once I went home. For me this was bad news because my birthday was three days away. On top of that, Spring quarter was going to start on March 26th.

Once I got home from surgery I couldn't really do too much of anything. I wasn't able to help around the house. I felt handicapped. It was very uncomfortable to have to lay down, get up, walk, sit, stand, or even just be, with this long nasty tube sticking out of my neck. To make it even worse, it was kind of painful. The surgeon prescribed Percocet to treat the pain but I have never liked taking pain pills, especially prescription strength. To be honest, I don't really trust medicine, or the medical industry. When I went in for my follow up the surgeon was surprised to hear that I had stopped taking the pills so soon when he offered to prescribe me more.

When my birthday rolled around, it was just another day. Although I couldn't celebrate I got phone calls and text messages from everyone wishing me a happy birthday. I talked to my mom a couple times that day. She told me she was going to send me some money for my birthday and she wanted to make sure I was doing ok following surgery. When I talked to her she didn't sound like she felt too good herself. I last spoke to her at around 4 p.m. and she told me she would call me back the next day.

Later on that night, at around 3 a.m., my phone rang. I didn't feel like getting up so I didn't. Then it rang again, I still didn't get up. The third time the phone rang Theresa answered it…

"Your mom's dead!", Theresa told me as she began crying.

I couldn't, and did not want to process what she was saying. My only reaction was to say "What?" then I yelled out "FUCK!". My step dad had only been gone less than a year. I could not afford to lose my mom. It was bad enough with her leaving to go live in California.

I grabbed the phone and my sister Yakini confirmed for me my worst nightmare. The woman who carried me in her womb, who breast fed me, she was gone. This woman who adored me, and did nothing but brag about me, she was gone. I lost a huge piece of myself. I lost something irreplaceable. You only get one mother. Despite all the hardship and all the suffering growing up, I would not have traded my mom for anyone. She was so kind hearted and so good to people. She was so willing to open up her home and take people in when they were in need of a place to stay.

Yes, my mom did suffer from crack cocaine addiction. Yes, her addiction did have a major negative impact on her parenting and her life in general. However, none of that changed the fact that she was an amazing woman who didn't have any enemies in the world. My mom was loved by everyone who encountered her. She always showed that same love right back. I could not believe she was gone. This was a day I had nightmares about, a day that I thought about constantly after my step-dad passed, a day that came way too soon.

My mom died in southern California. By the time she died, Nikki was already back in Washington. She had absolutely no family there for her. Me, Yakini, Nikki, and Sareeta did not have the money to pay to have her body transported back home. We tried raising money but had no luck whatsoever. Eventually, we ran out of time and our only option was, with the help of our aunts, to pay to have my mom cremated and then have her shipped back home in an urn. This meant that there would be no final goodbyes, there would be no viewing, there would be no open casket or even a casket period at her funeral. I felt so bad to not have the resources required to make sure my mom had a real funeral for the benefit of our family. However, that was just my reality. I was still trapped in poverty.

I believe in my heart that my mom only moved to California because she knew she was dying. She was in the house with her husband when he died and she knew how it felt to discover that his life was over and see his lifeless body. She knew how stressful it was for everyone when he was placed on hospice care. I feel like my mom thought she was doing us a favor. If this was what she was thinking then yes, she may have saved one of us from discovering her dead body. However, we would have loved to spend the last months of her life with her. I would have preferred to be able to cherish those final moments together. Either way, it was her decision to make. Unfortunately for me, there will always be a bit of mystery surrounding her death because when people who have illnesses such as diabetes and congestive heart failure suddenly die, there is no autopsy or investigation and no attempt to determine the actual cause of death. This combined with the fact that I never got to see her lifeless body means that in my mind anything could have happened to her. I'm probably better off having my final memory of her be with her full of life rather than lying in a coffin dead.

Despite the fact that I had just had surgery and lost the most important and special person to ever be in my life outside of my kids, life was not going to stop for me. The final quarter of my first year as a Washington Husky was going to start on March 26th no matter what. Time wouldn't be stopping for me.

On March 25^{th,} I had the tube removed from my neck, on March 26th, I was right back to working and taking classes. I was not going to let anything stop me at this point. My mom wanted me to be successful. She did not want to see me fail. I definitely wasn't going to allow her to be looking down on me and let her see that her death was the reason for me failing. Although I was tremendously, deeply, and irreparably hurt, I was also highly motivated. I have a gift when it comes to using tragedy to inspire triumph.

My mom's funeral was in early April. In place of a casket we had big pictures of her placed on easels with her urn in the middle on a stand. It was hard for me to keep my composure on the inside, but on the outside I put on a good act. I had to appear strong for my sisters. I couldn't let them see me broken. I also had to stay strong for my kids and all my nieces and nephews. In the end, despite us being together due to tragic circumstances, it ended up being a great send-off and a nice time with friends and family. After the funeral, all of the people between the ages of 21-35 came back to my house and we ate, drank, smoked weed, told stories, and had a good time.

Following my mom's death, my determination to be successful and climb out of poverty had hit an all-time high. I wanted to make sure that when I die, no one is burdened by my death. I want to make sure that I have a life insurance policy that will not only take care of all of my funeral expenses but also put some money in Theresa and my kid's pockets so they can make up for any lost wages or whatever financial need may arise, even if it's unrelated.

In my first two quarters at UW Tacoma, I had a 2.08 and a 2.90 gpa. In the quarter following my mom's death my gpa rose to a 3.5. If it weren't for the one credit/no credit class I took this quarter, I would have made the Dean's list for the first time as a Husky. In fact, following my mom's death, in my two worst quarters I had a 3.07 and a 3.45 gpa. Outside of those two quarters, I made the Dean's list every time.

Between the time of my mom's death and my graduation, life had been pretty steady for me without many major occurrences. Really, the only major occurrence following my mom's death and before I graduated was when I took a trip to Las Vegas and got off the plane to find out that my oldest son was in the hospital. He ultimately got diagnosed with a kidney disease called Minimal Change Disease which caused him to have what is called Nephrotic Syndrome.

It was very scary to find out that my child had a kidney disease. It honestly seemed like the medications that he was put on had far worse side effects than the symptoms of the disease. He was stuck taking medications for quite some time and had changes in his physical appearance and behavior as a result. The steroids that he was given come with warnings that kids should not use them for prolonged periods of time but the doctors kept him on it anyway. Eventually, we decided to ween him off and once we did all symptoms of the disease were gone and the side effects of the meds wore off as well.

I graduated with double bachelor's degrees in Psychology and Interdisciplinary Arts & Sciences: Self & Society in June of 2014. When I graduated, my mom couldn't be there to see it but I knew I made her proud. I knew she was looking down at me. However, my dad was there in the crowd to see me walk across the stage. I had other friends and family in attendance too and it was a very joyful occasion. However, once the graduation ceremony ended, life still had to go on. Graduating was not an instant ticket out of poverty.

I wasn't applying for jobs leading up to graduation and I honestly didn't know what I was going to do with my degrees. I have never liked being one of those people who maps out a path and follows it. I have always liked to be flexible and I prefer to go with the flow over planning. Obviously, there can be some situations where planning is necessary but for the most part I have always gotten by off improvising. This is what had gotten me to this point where I went from having a GED at the time of my release from prison to now having an Associate's degree and two Bachelor's degrees. Had I stuck to a plan I would have limited myself to being a drug and alcohol counselor.

One of my Psychology professors had seemed to take a special interest in my next step. She wanted to meet with me to talk about what I was going to do next. It was rare for me to have someone reach out to me wanting to help so I was very happy that she wanted to put time and effort into me and my future. I decided that I would go ahead and meet with her and see where it might take me.

When I met with her we discussed all kinds of things. We discussed my employment goals, her possible connections that could help me reach those goals, the possibility of having my record expunged, the idea of possibly co-writing an op-ed in the newspaper, and most importantly, grad school. After hearing about my goals and interests she thought that the Master of Social Work program would be a great fit for me. This was great news for me as I had a couple other people pushing me in that direction and I was highly interested in social work. I had also heard from students in that program that they loved what they were doing. I felt like my life experiences would have allowed me to make a huge impact as a social worker. She put me in touch with some of her contacts from the social work program to see what we could do.

When I contacted them I made sure to disclose my full criminal history so that there would be no surprises. What I heard back in response was extremely discouraging. One guy who I spoke with told me that several of my charges were permanently disqualifying from working with people who are part of vulnerable populations. He told me that meant it would be next to impossible for me to successfully land an internship which is required to complete the degree. I had mentioned in my e-mail that I hoped to reach a point at which my criminal history is no longer a factor and he flat out told me that no matter what I did, my criminal history would always be a factor. I felt like he overstepped his boundaries with those sorts of comments. He works at a university that encourages students to "be boundless".

Later on, I actually ended up speaking on a panel to faculty in the social work program about the experience of being a minority in graduate school at UW Tacoma and they were appalled when I shared this story with them. They told me that I definitely could have landed an internship and that people from backgrounds similar to mine should be encouraged to be social workers as they can relate to much of the population they would be serving and there is value to having diversity in the field. They were upset that I was discouraged from applying and many of them seemed ashamed of their colleague.

Once I received the bad news about my prospects of succeed at earning a Master's in Social Work, we keyed in on getting me accepted to the Master of Arts in Interdisciplinary Studies program. In order for me to apply, I needed to take the Graduate Record Examination (GRE), provide three letters of recommendation, and write a personal statement with my intended area of focus. For me, I figured that this was all going to be difficult.

For one, I didn't like the idea of having to take the GRE because math is one third of the exam. Second, outside of the professor who was helping me, I didn't have even one other person in mind who might write a letter of recommendation for me. Third, I had no idea what I wanted my area of focus to be in the graduate program. At first, these seemed like problems that would be very hard to overcome. In the end, it was no struggle at all to get through this process.

19
GRAD SCHOOL

Before applying to the graduate program I wanted to enroll in, I set up a meeting with the program advisor. When I met with her my confidence was boosted to the point where in my mind applying to the program would merely be a formality and I was going to get in no matter what. She told me that although I would be required to submit GRE scores, I should not waste time or money preparing to take the GRE. She told me they were far more concerned with other aspects of the application as opposed to the scores on this test. She also told me that it didn't matter too much who the letters of recommendation came from, I was not going to have to track down someone with power or pull, I could use pretty much anyone who could speak about my academic potential or accomplishments.

I ended up taking the GRE the following week. I scored a 152 on the verbal section, 147 on the quantitative, and a 5 on the analytical writing section. My verbal score placed me in the 54th percentile, my quantitative score placed me in the 28th percentile, and my analytical writing score placed me in the 93rd percentile. This means that out of 100 potential people headed to graduate school, 46 would have tested higher than me on the verbal side, 72 people would have tested higher than me on the quantitative side, and only 7 people would have tested higher than me on the analytic writing side. Keep in mind that this was with zero preparation and having no idea what to expect on the exam. I am very proud of my analytical writing score but I could do a lot better in the other areas although it doesn't surprise me that I am in the lower 30% of potential grad school students when it comes to math and numbers.

By the time I had taken the GRE, I also had made progress on getting letters of recommendation. I had sent out e-mails to several of my professors, many of which I only had for one class and never spoke to outside of class. I also sent an e-mail to my supervisor from my on-campus jobs. To my surprise, I had several people willing to write a letter of recommendation for me. I ended up getting the letters I needed from two professors who I had during the final quarter of my undergrad studies. They were both happy to help out and after hearing my story one of them told me I would be receiving her highest recommendation possible. I felt even more confident that I was going to be admitted to the program after securing these letters.

When writing my statement on my intended area of focus, I made it clear that I had a passion for helping people from disadvantaged backgrounds overcome their barriers to success. I wrote that I hoped to develop more direction and decide on a more specific area of focus as I progressed in the program. I had looked at the required courses and I figured that taking classes called Culture and Public Problems, or Evidence and Action, or Values and Action would open up my mind and lead me to my area of focus for my research.

The deadline to apply to the graduate program was in mid-August and I got everything in right on time. I was a couple months removed from finishing my undergrad studies and I wanted to make sure I had a backup plan just in case I wasn't accepted. I decided to apply for an AmeriCorps position training people for employment at Goodwill of Tacoma. Although working an AmeriCorps position is so low-paying that it's basically volunteer work, it comes with an extended grace period before my student loan payments would kick in and it also comes with a lump-sum payment toward those loans at the end.

I interviewed with AmeriCorps and a couple days later I was offered the position. I informed them that I would accept the position, however, if I was accepted into graduate school they would need to utilize their backup choice. Although I had thoughts about doing both grad school and AmeriCorps, I figured I could be setting myself up for failure as they both involve large time commitments equivalent to a full-time job. I had a tough decision to make because not long after being offered the AmeriCorps position, I received my acceptance letter for graduate school.

This was a major moment in my life. When I got out of prison I had the goal of transforming my failure into success but I had no idea that it would lead me here. I had no idea that graduate school was in the cards for me. A Master's degree? Really? Me? This was an opportunity that I was not going to allow to slip away.

Although I was excited, I was a little bit worried about entering graduate school. From time to time, I would second guess myself and wonder if I really belonged in college period. If I had to wonder if I belonged in college, those concerns would be even worse in grad school. I heard that only 10%

of Americans have a graduate degree. I wonder how many amongst that 10% were also high school dropouts? How many were convicted felons who spent time in prison? How many of them are even black?

Regardless of any concerns, I had gotten accepted, and I was ready to begin this next stage of my transformation. Fall quarter 2014 started at the end of September. I was enrolled in a class called Models & Critical Inquiry, as well as a class called Culture & Public Problems.

Models & Critial Inquiry was all about learning words such as paradigm, espistemology, axiology, ontology and a bunch of other words I had either never heard or never paid attention to before. It was also geared toward introducing us to various ways of viewing research and the world. The overall goal was to teach us about the research process and how our research question should be the key to determining our approaches.

Culture & Public Problems was all about how cultural factors play a role in how we frame things as being problematic. In this class we looked at how two media outlets, for example, might write about the same exact story utilizing shockingly different tones and language that shape how the public will interpret that story. Unfortunately, the professor decided that we should focus on climate change as opposed to some of the topics that I would have found more interesting in a community and social change program such as issues impacting people from disadvantaged backgrounds. The program has a social justice focus so I expected a class called Culture & Public Problems to be focused on problems within the inner city, racism, discrimination, homelessness, things along that line but instead we spent our time reading and writing about climate change. I wrote my final paper and presentation about why people like me from the inner-city who come from disadvantage backgrounds don't rank environmental issues very highly in terms of social problems. It's not that the environment isn't important but when you have to hustle every day to get by and you are constantly in survival mode, environmental concerns most likely won't be on your radar.

I wasn't able to get through my first month of grad school before tragedy struck my family again. My dad and uncle were looking for a place to stay together and they had found one but my uncle couldn't find my dad to sign the paperwork. By this point my dad had all kinds of health issues resulting from many years of alcohol and drug abuse. My dad used to have Old English 800 malt liquor for breakfast, lunch, dinner, and snack. All the years of doing this had taken its toll. My dad also was very stubborn and wanted to live on his own terms so he didn't care what any doctors had to say about his lifestyle.

My dad had been told that he might have some sort of blood cancer. He was told he didn't have long to live years prior, even before my step-dad had passed. He didn't pay the doctors who told him that any mind and he continued living life on his terms. He had undergone several blood transfusions and spent a lot of time in the hospital leading up to this point. He was in a lot of pain and was beginning to struggle with simple things such as standing and sitting. Although my dad was an alcoholic, he was the type of person who always woke up early and made it a point to leave the house and try to maximize his day. He loved being on the move. It was tough for me to see him struggling physically.

About a week before he went missing I had taken him to a Mariners game along with my son and my nephew. It was very hard for him to walk into the stadium. He struggled to get to the seats and kept needing to stop. When we left he had to wait at the corner right outside of Safeco Field for me to navigate through the crowd and pick him up. It was obvious he was in really bad shape but he didn't like going to the doctor unless he absolutely had to.

Once it became clear that my uncle was worried about my dad I became worried too. I began to call hospitals to make sure he wasn't there. With Harborview being the a popular hospital in Seattle I made sure to call them. However, when I called them they told me they didn't have a patient by my dad's name.

Eventually, more time went by and no one had heard from my dad. Finally, on the 21st of October, we found out where he was. Apparently, on October 10th, 911 was called to where my dad was living and he was taken by ambulance to Harborview. My dad remained at Harborview from October 10th until October 16th, which is when he passed away. This means that my dad lied there dead at Harborview for five whole days before we found out. He was there alive for six days, and we knew nothing. Harborview had absolutely no explanation as to why no one in our family had been contacted. Not only should we have been contacted once he passed away, we should have been contacted while he was still alive.

I was once again devastated to suffer a very close loss. All three of the people who raised me were now dead. I wasn't a child but I felt like an orphan. First Fred, then my mom, now my dad? When would it stop? When would I get a break? I did not want to have to plan or attend another funeral, but I had no choice.

I found out that my dad had died early in the morning. A couple hours later, I was supposed to be at a job interview for a student assistant position in the financial aid office at the University of Washington Tacoma. After that, I had a meeting with one of my professors, then after that I was supposed to go to class. Despite having my heart crushed, I decided that I was not going to skip these things. I needed to keep myself busy. Additionally, I need this job. I also didn't want to suffer any setbacks in school.

I showed up to the job interview as planned and I held myself together pretty well. I planned on not even mentioning the fact that my dad had died because I didn't want to get the job due to pity and I also didn't want it to seem like I had too much going on in my life to where they didn't want to give me the job. However, toward the end of the interview, I brought up the fact that I had just heard my dad died that morning. The lady who interviewed me was shocked that I had the resiliency to still show up and she ended up giving me the job.

When I met with my professor I talked with her for a bit before the subject of my dad's passing came up. She looked at me like I was crazy for being there and I explained to her that I didn't want to fall behind or miss any requirements. She gave me a big hug and told me not to worry about any of that and suggested I go be with my family. She also told me that she "better not" see me in class later that night. I was somewhat relieved and happy to have such support.

My dad was not a religious man at all. He was an atheist. The only time you would hear him speak about religion is if he was making a joke about it or mocking it. I knew that he would not want to have his funeral at a church with people preaching about God and Heaven but ultimately we decided that a funeral is more about the family and loved ones seeking closure rather than what the deceased may have wanted. My dad always told us that if he dies we should just throw him in the bushes somewhere. He had way too many people who loved and cared about him for that.

Although we still didn't have any money, and my dad didn't have insurance, he had a friend who worked at a funeral home. She agreed to transport his body to Portland where his mom, brothers, and sisters live so we could have a service and do his cremation for a low price. Also, my aunt found a church that was willing to host his service and she took care of all the food for afterwards. My cousin TT paid for the transport, embalming, and cremation initially and we managed to give her most of the money back. I had to use student loan money in order to chip in.

Despite the fact that my dad didn't work for a large majority of my life and he spent a lot of time as a transient, I never felt more proud to be his son than I did at his funeral. Hearing people credit him for inspiring them to pursue an education or somehow making them feel good about themselves made me feel good and proud to share his name. Hearing stories about his days as a leader of the Portland Black Panthers re-iterated to me the history and value of being named after such a man. Just like I would never want to replace my mom with any other mother, I could also never replace my dad with any other father. They both struggled mightily as parents but they were victims of a war that was waged against us. Crack cocaine ruining people and communities of color was no accident.

Once the funeral was over with it was time to start my new job and zone in on graduate school. Once again, I didn't allow myself to break down or slip in any way. I stayed strong because it was all I knew how to do. I felt like if I could make it through these deaths, I could make it through anything. I finished my first quarter of grad school with a 3.7 in both classes which boosted my confidence and provided me with evidence that I was not in over my head being a graduate student.

As I progressed in my graduate program I keyed in on a potential research topic. I had identified a chair for my committee and decided that my area of research would be on the educational impacts for children who live in low-income public housing. I had hypothesized that kids served by low-income public housing agencies would be enrolled in lower-funded and poorer performing schools which would therefore lead to negative academic impacts and lower performance. This hypothesis was based on the project-like conditions that a lot of kids live in as well as the lower property values and lower property taxes being paid. This area of research was largely inspired by my personal experiences living in low-income public housing, not only as a student, but also as a parent.

As I dug deeper into this topic my interest in it waned. Communication with the chair I had identified had stopped completely. She is the type of professor who works well with students who have it all together and know exactly what they want to do but that wasn't quite where I was. I needed a bit more time to develop my approach and direction. Plus, I felt like while this was an important topic, it wasn't something that I was super passionate about. It was definitely in line with my values, but I didn't know if I could go all in with this topic. It didn't have the grasp on my mind that I wanted my thesis or project to have. I felt like I would do the best work if I identified an area of focus that could lead to some sort of ground-breaking and life-changing project. I wanted to be able to really make an impact.

As time went by, I continued making progress in my program and completing all of the core classes. However, I wasn't getting anywhere in terms of forming a full committee with both a chair and a reader or completing research so I could write my thesis or project. This was one of those situations where I didn't have a lot of guidance and I didn't fully understand how things worked. Had I been privileged enough to have family, friends, mentors, or role models who had been through this before I may have been motivated to be more decisive and begin my research much sooner than I had. I did not have my chair and topic firmly in place until the quarter before I should have been graduating and it wasn't until what should have been my final quarter of the program when I finally had my full committee formed and my exact project goal determined.

For most students, that would delay them tremendously or even lead to them not completing their degree. That is what some students who came in the program before me had went through. However, for me, it was for the most part smooth sailing once I had keyed in on a specific project that I was passionate about. Also, the graduate program ultimately recognized that they needed to be more pro-active in making sure students make progress and I hear that they made the necessary changes to help get students going on these things much sooner.

After considering switching my focus from Community & Social Change to Non-profit leadership, I decided that my research would be on the impact that post-secondary education has on preventing recidivism. Recidivism is when a person is sent to prison for committing a crime, released, and then they commit a new crime that sends them back to prison. Post-secondary education is when an individual pursues an education past the high school level such as technical school, community college, or a university.

I hypothesized that post-secondary educational achievement could have a positive impact on reducing the risk for recidivism. I believed this mostly because it had been playing out in my life. I had personally seen a transformation take place in my life in which I went from spending every day committing crimes and chasing money to living my life with a positive focus and direction. This was a topic that I could really get into. This was something that would allow me to not only utilize my own personal life experiences but I could also use this as an opportunity to have an impact on bettering the lives of people with backgrounds like mine.

20
MASTER OF ADVERSITY

When Winter quarter of 2016 began, I was at the end of the road in grad school in terms of core classes, but at the very beginning in terms of completing a thesis or project so I could graduate. A thesis requires you to make a scholarly contribution in your area of research but a project can be something that allows you to immediately implement your research to make a difference, so I wanted to complete a project. The beginning of this quarter is when I finally made up my mind on a topic and began the research.

I was registered for two classes this quarter, one was a Graduate Research and Writing class, the other was called Evidence & Action. Both are core classes in my graduate program. In my Evidence & Action class there was only one other student which made for an awkward quarter, however, it allowed for a lot of interaction with the professor. I ended up asking her if she would be the chair on my committee for my project and she agreed. In the Graduate Research & Writing class we were required to lay the foundation for either our thesis or our project rationale and this forced me to make a lot of progress.

In this class we were required to write our introduction, literature review, methods section, analysis/results section, and our conclusion. This was a large chunk of our full project or thesis. By the time this course was scheduled to be over, I would have had the majority of my project rationale written. This, along with the fact that I had my chair, gave me great hope of finishing my degree by the end of Summer quarter. While that would be one quarter late, it still would have taken me less than two full calendar years to earn my Master's degree.

I began reading a lot about mass incarceration. I learned a lot about racial disparities within the criminal justice system. Most importantly, I learned that researchers had been coming to the conclusion that post-secondary education does indeed reduce the risk for recidivism. I found opportunity in the fact that most research that came to this conclusion was based on prison-based post-secondary educational programs. There is a large gap in the research whereas the experiences of formerly incarcerated people, who attend college post-release, have not been studied.

In order to address this gap in the research I chose a research method called Autoethnography. Autoethnography makes the researcher the focus of the research. My research process involved writing about and analyzing my personal experiences as a formerly incarcerated college student. In order to make this an impactful project, as opposed to a thesis, I analyzed my experiences with the intention of developing the curriculum and an accompanying workbook for a college preparatory workshop for formerly incarcerated people.

I had finally found my niche. I found an important area to focus on that I was passionate about. This was a topic that I saw myself becoming an expert on. I figured that this was something that would not only earn me a Master's degree, but it could potentially lead to a career. All it took was for me to be motivated and have a sense of direction and getting the work done would be no issue for me.

The chair of my committee had recommended a potential reader from the education program. I felt that he was a great fit and he was down to join the team. The very first day I met him, he began connecting me with people who could help me with making my project a reality. He referred me to a woman at Tacoma Community College who he had worked with and before I could get half the work done on my project I already had an outlet with funding that was willing to pay me to bring my workshop there. Everything had seemed to fall in place perfectly.

Unfortunately, this is me we are talking about here. Nothing in my life has ever come easy. There wasn't any way I was going to go from having no sense of direction to earning my degree without some sort of unfortunate circumstances or setbacks. It was only a matter of time before things started to go bad for me.

During Spring quarter I had gotten a lot of work done. I was taking a Capstone class that required us to take those same components that we had created in the Graduate Research & Writing class and turn it into high quality graduate level work. We shared our work with our peers and receive feedback in addition to received feedback and comments from the professor, who was also the head of the program.

I received nothing but positive feedback from both my peers and the professor. At times, they made me feel very good about my work. I never had much to change or alter based on their suggestions. However, when my committee had to read and provide feedback on these same documents the response was very different. I began to get the sense that the three of us, me, my chair, and my reader, were not on the same page.

For example, before I started the Capstone class my chair had to approve me being in the class. The only way I would be let in was if I completed the research process and was ready to write. We came to an agreement on what that meant, and I did what I had to do, so I was let in the class. However, a couple weeks into the Capstone class, my reader finally got around to providing feedback on a document I had sent him a month prior and he was confused about many aspects of my research process. This lead to my chair going back on many things she had previously said in terms of what stage I was at and I was back to working on parts of my project that I was told I was done with. One of the most frustrating aspects of this was being asked to engage with theories that played no role in anything I had done up until that point which is essentially the same as starting over if you are going to approach the research from a new lens.

Ultimately, I ended up telling my committee that I had too many voices involved and that we needed to take a step back. I was being told by my peers and my current professor that I was doing great work. I felt like I was doing great work. I was being told that everything made sense and it was clear that I had a firm grasp on what I was doing. When I would later have that contradicted by the people who had to sign off on my degree that was not a good feeling so I decided that we should stop engaging until I was done with the Capstone. Once I made it through this final class then I could meet any final requirements they had of me once Summer quarter started and I was enrolled in project credits and working only with them.

Between the Graduate Research & Writing class and Capstone I made more progress in two quarters than anyone can realistic expect to make. I went from having nothing to having a full project rationale and the curriculum complete. I also had begun making strides in creating the workbook.

I began to realize that I was being held to a much different standard by my committee than what was necessary and a much different standard than my peers. Initially, I didn't mind because I was all for making sure my work was of the highest quality. Eventually, I came to realize that there didn't seem to be much validity to what they wanted me to do. My project, as I mentioned, was to utilize Autoethnography as a method to analyze my personal experiences for the creation of the curriculum and workbook for a workshop. Autoethnography is an established qualitative research method. It seemed as if my committee was not going to be satisfied unless I found another scholar who had utilized autoethnography to develop a workshop just as I was doing which made no sense considering that this was a unique project. They wanted me to justify using this method and approach in a way that none of my classmates were being required to justify their work. While justification of any scholarly approach is necessary, scholarly work is not only validated through finding prior scholars who have done things the exact same way. That is a way to clip the wings of students and kill innovation. However, they were the ones who had to sign off on my degree so I wanted to do whatever it took to satisfy them.

Once I completed Capstone, the remaining requirements for me to earn my Master's degree were to earn 10 project credits, complete my project rationale, and complete the curriculum and workbook that made up my actual project. Considering all the progress I had made the previous two quarters, I had no doubt that I could complete these tasks by the end of Summer. I informed the chair of my committee that I intended to participate in the hooding and commencement ceremony with the class of 2016. In order to participate, students have to be earning their degree by the end of Summer quarter.

Although I was not all the way at the finish line it felt amazing to be able to register for commencement. The day when I picked up my cap, gown, and hood was a great day for me. This would be my third graduation ceremony, however, this one was by far the most special. I felt extremely blessed to have come so far from being that young kid with no guidance who dropped out of school. However, thinking about my loved ones who weren't here to witness it was a source of deep pain.

My sister Nikki had spent the prior three months leading to my hooding ceremony and commencement hospitalized. Due to her diabetes and congestive heart failure, her body was hardly functioning any more. She had undergone a very high risk heart procedure at the University of Washington Medical Center in Seattle and survived, but she was still not doing very well and couldn't go home.

This was a very stressful situation for me. Some of the worst experiences of my life are listening to doctors and nurses tell my loved ones that they are basically on the verge of death. It was very hard to watch my sister be taken back for a procedure that they were warning could take her life, and it was even more difficult to see the level of depression and sadness she had to deal with.

After several months in the hospital, she was sent to a run-down and unprofessional nursing home that was supposed to be helping her rehabilitate and gain strength so she could go home. Although this place made her very miserable, it was good for her to be back in Tacoma and closer to her loved ones. UW Medical Center was over an hour drive for us but the nursing home she was moved to was only 15 minutes from my house. When she first got there she was so happy to be out of the hospital and one step closer to going home.

Being hospitalized for so long probably feels far worse than being in jail. It must have felt great for her to go outside for a walk in her wheelchair. I had pushed her across the street to Fred Meyer so she could buy some things and we went to McDonalds. She seemed happy for the first time in a long time. Theresa was pregnant with twin girls at the time and Nikki used to always remind me about when I would say I only make boys. She always talked about how she couldn't wait to meet my twins.

With Nikki being out of the hospital and in the nursing home I thought there was a possibility that she could attend my hooding ceremony and commencement but it didn't happen. She seemed upset that she couldn't be there but she was proud of my accomplishment. I participated in the hooding in front of my kids, my sisters, a couple of my aunts, Theresa, and Theresa's mom and grandma. Everyone was so proud and happy for me. I got a lot of questions about how it felt but my response was always that I'm not quite done yet.

Shortly after the hooding ceremony, the commencement ceremony took place. I ended up stuck in traffic and arrived an hour late. Ironically, being late put me in the unique position of being the very first student in line to walk out amongst every member of the class of 2016. My program happened to be leading the way and was at the front of the line. When I arrived they were just about to begin the ceremony and the only place I could fit was at the very front of the line. It was a little awkward being the first student because I knew I wouldn't just blend in with the crowd but at the same time I couldn't ignore the significance of coming from where I come from, and going through what I have went through, to leading a very large group of college graduates from the back room where we gather to our seats. As Pop and Circumstance glared over the Tacoma Dome speakers, I proudly led the group of grads to our seats while waving to the crowd and scanning for my loved ones.

Once the ceremony was over and all the congratulations and handshakes were handed out, it was time to finish earning my degree. I have heard stories about students who have participated in commencement and hooding ceremonies but then never actually graduated. There is a major difference between commencement and graduation. If you had to choose one over the other, graduation would be the choice 100% of the time. Commencement is the ceremony, graduating means completing all your requirements and earning your degree.

I had spent my whole time as a graduate student working in the financial aid office at UWT. This was the best and most beneficial job I had ever held.

I worked with nothing but cool people and the experience of serving students is something I cannot possibly replace. Nothing felt better than to have a student walk in to the financial aid office wanting to talk to a counselor and being able to assist the student without having to bother the counselors. I gained experience working with the most diverse group of students imaginable. I was very grateful for my time as an employee in this office but it was time for that to come to an end.

The main reason I felt the need to leave my job was because I wanted to put all of my time and effort into finishing my degree. I would not want to limit the amount of work on my project I could complete due to having to work around my shifts in the financial aid office. In addition to needing to complete my degree, a policy had changed which led to the student workers being required to complete background checks. The idea of having a background check ran on me after already working in the office for so long didn't sit well with me. I had given presentations on campus disclosing my criminal history and made no attempts to hide anything but I felt like the background check was going to lead to them letting me go anyway.

A few days before Summer quarter started, Nikki had a stroke and was sent back to the hospital. The stroke caused her to become blind in one eye. After a day or so at the hospital she was sent back to the nursing home. During this transition, somehow the nursing home forgot to schedule her dialysis appointment. Had she stayed in the hospital she would have received it there but since she was returned to the nursing home it was their responsibility to schedule an appointment and make sure she got there. I went to the nursing home and I asked if a grievance could be filed about the mistake because when it comes to these types of appointments, it is a life or death situation.

While I was there, Nikki broke down crying, telling me she was miserable and didn't even want to live any more. She felt like she was trapped in a mental institution. The nursing home she was at had a large population of people with mental health issues and some of them had very disturbing behaviors. I joked around with her and told her she had gone crazy and was in a mental institution and although it got a laugh out of her, she was very serious. She told the people at the nursing home to stay in contact with me and that I was going to be the one taking care of her and handling her grievance. I gave her a hug and a kiss and went on my way.

Summer quarter started on June 20th, 2016. I was set up to meet with my committee for a discussion about moving forward with whatever requirements they had for me that first week of the quarter. I had no idea what to expect from the meeting as I was already frustrated by the way things were going. A part of me wanted to make a change but it was very late to do that and would put my graduation at risk.

Unfortunately, on the morning of June 21st, I got a call informing me that my sister had passed away at the nursing home. I felt sick. I was sad, furious, and defeated all at the same time. Out of all of the losses I had recently dealt with, this was the hardest one. My sister did not die in her 50s or 60s, she was only 37 years old. She left behind a 9 year-old-son who also had an absent father. As bad as I felt myself, I knew that this had to be even harder for her son. He had to go through seeing his mom stuck in the hospital and nursing home and then ultimately found out she was never coming home. I felt so bad for him.

When it came time for me to meet with my committee, I didn't even show up. I was trying to plan yet another funeral, and I also had taken in my nephew. Life was very hard at the time and the last thing I could think about was school work. When my chair had e-mailed me asking why I didn't show up I informed her that my sister passed and she told me to take the time I needed.

We struggled once again to arrange and pay for a funeral service and cremation but we made it happen. There was a lot more financial support coming in when my sister died compared to everyone else I had lost. I was tasked with making the arrangements with the funeral home and planning everything out and it was really a drain on me. There had been times when I visited my sister in the hospital and she told me to make sure that her medical situation wasn't causing me to do bad in school. I knew that I had to keep pushing forward. It wasn't going to be easy, but I had to do it. The funeral was done and over with, and it was time to get back to business. I could not stop.

When I was finally able to meet with my chair it angered me that she brought up the fact that I had missed a meeting with her. She even had the nerve to tell me that "I get one freebie". I couldn't believe the level of insensitivity. I had just lost one of the most important people in my life, someone who helped take care of me when my parents didn't, someone who was irreplaceable. In addition to this, she was stuck on the idea that I wasn't going to graduate after Summer quarter and needed to be engaging with theories that had nothing to do with my project. I felt like I was ready to complete the actual project but she had me stuck on the rationale. Ultimately, she presented me with a list of things I needed to complete and I spent the quarter meeting all of her requirements.

Toward the middle of the quarter I was invited to attend a conference for people who work with individuals re-entering society following a prison sentence called the CPTS Summer Institute. This was a great opportunity to speak with people about the workshop I was creating. I wanted to network with as many people as possible and take full advantage of any connections I could make. However, two hours into the 3-day conference, I got a call that Theresa had gone into labor.

My twin baby girls were born on July 27th, 2016. After having four kids I thought I would be done but God had other plans for me. Previously, all three of my biological kids were boys. Although our oldest was a girl and I had been in her life since she was in diapers, I didn't actually have a daughter of my own. I never really wanted one. Every time Theresa had gotten pregnant I hoped it was a boy and that was true with the twins as well. Ultimately, I feel extremely blessed to have my little girls.

My ambitious goal of graduating after Summer quarter was simply not in the cards for me. I was having issues with my committee and I had to deal with the death of my sister. Taking in my nephew and the birth of my twin daughters during the quarter also had a major impact. We went from having four kids in the house to having seven in a real short period of time and that made school work a little hard to do. I still did what I had to do but I wasn't able to go above and beyond as I had done in the previous quarters.

I was going to have to wait until the end of Fall quarter to finally be done with school after so many years. I didn't really mind the fact that it was going to take another quarter as I knew there was not a lot of work left for me to do. I could go ahead and register for additional project credits in the Fall and I'd be done by December. I had addressed all of my committee's concerns so it should be smooth sailing from there.

However, when I submitted my work at the end of the quarter I was informed by my chair that I would receive an incomplete grade. I didn't understand why this was necessary despite me meeting every single requirement set for me. The honest truth was she had to give me an incomplete because she didn't have time to review my work due to other responsibilities. Incompletes are typically for students who still had work that had not yet been turned in, but would be turned in at a later date leading to a grade change. Although my project was not complete, only half of it was supposed to be done in order for me to receive the 10 project credits I had registered for per our agreement that we both signed.

I had put in a lot of work during one of the toughest periods of my life and it was a slap in the face to be told I wouldn't receive credit. Especially without her even reviewing the work. When I was told I was getting an incomplete I marched out of the door and immediately contacted the head of my program in an attempt to figure out how to proceed with forming a new committee. I had no idea what would happen but I felt like I had no choice but to take this drastic step.

When I made this move it was a dangerous, but necessary one. I got extremely lucky when the head of the program decided that he would be my chair. He was my professor in Capstone so he was familiar with my work already. It was a perfect fit and a smooth transition. He also identified a reader which saved me from that difficult task. I am extremely grateful to him for making this transition go so smoothly. I was presented with a list of requirements that I needed to complete and while he did want to me to change my tone in a couple places on my project rationale, he put me in a position where I could focus on completing the curriculum and workbook that make up my project.

At the end of Fall quarter I had done everything I needed to do and my new committee signed off on my Master's degree. This stage of my life was finally over. After 8 long years of hard work I had succeeded in going from a GED to a Master's degree. I was very excited to be done, but still worried about my future. I was in a unique position to use my research project to help other people with a history of incarceration do the same thing, however, I still needed to be given an opportunity to make that happen.

21
PROGRESSION

While still a student at UW Tacoma, I was connected with people at Tacoma Community College who were interested in paying me to facilitate my workshop on their campus. I had several meetings with them over a long period of time and we did an excellent job getting the word out to various people at organizations that work in the field of re-entry. Despite our efforts, no one showed up at the workshop.

A lot of college graduates immediately begin looking for a job so they can support themselves and their family. When you have an entrepreneurial mindset, as I do, looking for a job is a last resort. I formed a sole proprietorship under the name Progression, which is the name of my workshop, and I intend to get my own business going. If I am not able to succeed with my own company, then I will begin looking for traditional employment. Although I now have built a resume and hold several college degrees, there are still barriers related to obtaining employment if that is the route I end up going.

In one of my graduate classes we had to read about the difference between a job, a career, and a calling. Each one of these three types of employment typically involve a specific type of motivation. These motivations and related values will ultimately determine which path an individual takes with their life.

People who have a job are motivated by money. They are trading their hours for money and the paycheck is their primary driving force. People who have a career are motivated by a desire to advance and climb the ladder in addition to being motivated by their paycheck. People who have a calling, however, are intrinsically motivated. These people have something that they are passionate about and willing to sacrifice for and their motivations are internally driven by their values.

I could easily settle for a job, if they are willing to look past my criminal history, and begin trading time for money to support my family. However, I don't see this making me happy for very long. I don't see accepting a job as building a foundation. There wouldn't be much room for advancement and I wouldn't be very happy stuck in the same place for very long.

A career is definitely enticing to me. I would love to be able to make an honest living while also having room for growth and opportunity within the same field or company. This is a possibility for me, however, as with a job, there are barriers based on my criminal history and relative lack of professional experience.

Ideally, I would make a living out of pursuing my calling. I believe that I have been called to make a difference in the lives of people who come from disadvantaged backgrounds. Especially people whose disadvantaged backgrounds led to them being incarcerated. I feel like it was not by chance that my academic journey played out the way it did and led me down a path in which I used a research method that analyzed my own experiences with the intention of helping people like me. While there are many organizations and institutions that could allow me to pursue my calling, the best way would be to design and implement my own programs and interventions while being my own boss free from policies and restrictions that kill innovation.

In a perfect world, I would be teaching at a community college while facilitating workshops, publishing books, guides and manuals related to overcoming disadvantaged backgrounds, and doing public speaking engagements. While teaching at a community college could be viewed as either a job or career, I consider it to be part of my calling. My post-secondary educational journey began at the community college level and I feel like I can make a very positive impact in that setting. If I were to teach a class or two per quarter that would allow me time to pursue the other interests I mentioned through my own company.

No matter what, I see my future as being very bright. I am committed and I feel like I am in position to make an impact. As I help more and more people succeed and overcome their barriers, the impact will lead to more opportunities. I honestly believe in my heart that as long as my values stay intact and I place the people I serve before profits or other selfish desires, money will follow. I might have to do a lot of work for free as I build a reputation within the re-entry community but in the end it will pay off.

Growing up in poverty led to my values being all messed up. I was too busy trying to live up to what I heard in rap songs and saw on TV. I figured that the only way to be successful in life was to be rich. I didn't have anyone around showing me any different. My experience of being incarcerated and away from my kids provided me with all of the motivation in the world to replace those messed up values with new and more positive ones. Becoming an educated grown man provided me with the knowledge and experience required to replace those values. I have learned that I don't have to be rich to be successful or happy. I don't have to become a millionaire. I don't have to chase that next big lick. The best rewards and the best things in life are not financial.

Although I made a ton of money during my life of crime, my life was not great. It was an illusion when I perceived having a nice car on rims with a gold chain as being the good life. The good life involves spending time with family and friends, doing good for your community, and developing a positive image and reputation. When you spend your time doing positive things and you keep a positive attitude that is what leads to a positive and happy life.

Since turning my life around, blessing upon blessing has come my way. I have dealt with a ton of unfortunate circumstances but at the same time I can't take my blessings for granted. It seems like as long as I keep progressing and refuse to turn back to my old ways, God will not allow me to fail. I have never been a religious person but I am a strong believer in God. I would not be here today if it were not for the grace of God. I would have never been able to come this far.

I am being used as a vessel to deliver a message to the disadvantaged that we do not need to settle or sell ourselves short. Even those of us who society locked away and stripped rights away from should be seen for our potential as opposed to our risks. A criminal history does not preclude anyone from being a positive and productive member of society.

In order for people like me to reach our full potential it requires cooperation from society. We need to stop being denied opportunities to make a living and put a roof over our families' heads. We need to be included in conversations about ways to best address issues involving us. We need to have people who have made it out of poverty or turned their life around serve as mentors to those whose transitions are just getting started.

We need policies and practices in place that make successful re-integration back into society as barrier-free as possible. A ton of money is spent on incarcerating people, why don't we take a large chuck of that money and invest it into non-profits and other organizations that work in the field of re-entry and stop people from coming back? The majority of people released from jail or prison will return, causing a huge burden on the tax-payers. It is far more beneficial to spend that money creating jobs, housing and opportunities to ensure that they become tax-paying citizens and don't return to incarceration.

I am writing this final section of this book on January 20th, 2017, the day that Donald J. Trump replaced Barack Obama as President of the United

States of America. We are entering a scary time in history. The change in office could potentially lead to the return of "tough on crime" legislation that makes life harder for formerly incarcerated people and people from disadvantaged backgrounds who get in trouble with the law. We also may see large scale changes in education funding and opportunities as a result of this new administration taking power.

Regardless of our political opinions or affiliations the future has not been written yet. Full control of the future is in our hands. We need to make sure that people who care are in positions to make sure that stories like mine are a thing of the past. While my transformation has been great, it should have never been necessary.

Parents who struggle with raising their children should not be ignored or punished, they should be assisted. People who suffer from addictions and mental illness should have all of the support and resources that they need. People with serious medical conditions should be educated and trained to properly manage their condition before it becomes deadly. Kids who are showing signs of being at risk of dropping out should be a priority and have interventions in place that make it harder to not succeed than it is to succeed.

A lot of different factors and circumstances played a role in shaping my attitudes, beliefs, and behaviors that made me a part of that school-to-prison pipeline where I became a dropout and convicted felon. This began for me as a child. Ultimately, none of those factors were within my control. I was failed. I was failed not only by my parents, I was failed by society.

Whenever a child has drug-addicted parents who receive no help, society has failed that child. Whenever a child is expelled from public school and especially through no fault of his own, society has failed that child. Whenever, a child is allowed to stop attending school in the 6th grade with no one reaching out to help or ask what's wrong, society has failed that child.

Society failed to protect and take care of me during my youth. It has been said that it takes a village to raise a child but where was my village? When that village is absent, values get distorted, priorities get lost, and childhoods like mine take place.

It took for me to be in college for me to locate that village. It took for me to be in college before any person outside of my family took an interest in me and saw me as someone with potential who was worth guiding. It took a miracle for me to be in college.

I am living proof that people and their attitudes and behaviors are largely shaped by their life circumstances. It is very easy to look at the actions of other people and judge them, wondering how they could do such things or behave in such a way, but until you have walked a mile in their shoes, you are not qualified to judge. The well-off people of the world would have to be in the position of the thief to know whether or not they would have done anything differently. However, it is safe to say that if the petty thief was in the position of well-off people there would be no motivation or desire to be a petty thief. This is not to say that socio-economic status determines who are good and bad people, but rather, I am saying that life circumstances play a major role in shaping people and determining values and behavior.

Once I became a college student and began to view myself through a positive lens my life was transformed. All of the negative views and labels that I had acquired were replaced with a new positive self-image. All of my negative experiences in school growing up were replaced with more positive experiences in college. The crime and every day hustle that was a large part of who I was got replaced by the everyday grind of being a college student and student worker. Getting good grades and positive feedback played a major role in boosting my self-esteem. Achieving a post-secondary education, for me, was a way to transform society's failure and lay a foundation for future generations of my family.

CPSIA information can be obtained
at www.ICGtesting.com
Printed in the USA
LVOW07s2310081017
551718LV00006B/130/P